Getting Started with Qt 5

Introduction to programming Qt 5 for cross-platform
application development

Benjamin Baka

BIRMINGHAM - MUMBAI

Getting Started with Qt 5

Commissioning Editor: Pavan Ramchandani
Acquisition Editor: Siddharth Mandal
Content Development Editor: Mohammed Yusuf Imaratwale
Technical Editor: Surabhi Kulkarni
Copy Editor: Safis Editing
Project Coordinator: Pragati Shukla
Proofreader: Safis Editing
Indexer: Tejal Daruwale Soni
Graphics: Alishon Mendonsa
Production Coordinator: Jisha Chirayil

First published: February 2019

Production reference: 1280219

Published by Packt Publishing Ltd.
Livery Place
35 Livery Street
Birmingham
B3 2PB, UK.

ISBN 978-1-78995-603-0

www.packtpub.com

`mapt.io`

Mapt is an online digital library that gives you full access to over 5,000 books and videos, as well as industry leading tools to help you plan your personal development and advance your career. For more information, please visit our website.

Why subscribe?

- Spend less time learning and more time coding with practical eBooks and Videos from over 4,000 industry professionals

- Improve your learning with Skill Plans built especially for you

- Get a free eBook or video every month

- Mapt is fully searchable

- Copy and paste, print, and bookmark content

Packt.com

Did you know that Packt offers eBook versions of every book published, with PDF and ePub files available? You can upgrade to the eBook version at `www.packt.com` and as a print book customer, you are entitled to a discount on the eBook copy. Get in touch with us at `customercare@packtpub.com` for more details.

At `www.packt.com`, you can also read a collection of free technical articles, sign up for a range of free newsletters, and receive exclusive discounts and offers on Packt books and eBooks.

Contributors

About the author

Benjamin Baka is a full-stack software developer and is passionate about cutting-edge technologies and elegant programming techniques. He has 10 years in different technologies, from C++, Java, Ruby, Python to Qt. Some of the projects he's working on can be found on his GitHub page. He is currently working on exciting technologies all from the camp of mPedigree Network.

I'd like to thank the Baka family for all of their support in my many endeavors. Another thanks to Samuel Afari for encouraging me to go beyond my limits.

To the entire Packt team, it's been a pleasure working with you.

And I continue to stay forever indebted to Guido Sohne and Lorenzo Cabrini for their amazing guidance and input in my life.

About the reviewer

Nibedit Dey is a techno-entrepreneur and innovator with over 8 years of experience in building complex software-based products using Qt and C++. Before starting his entrepreneurial journey, he worked for L&T and Tektronix in different research and development roles. Additionally, he has reviewed *The Modern C++ Challenge, Hands-on GUI programming with C++ and Qt5,* and *Hands-On High Performance Programming with Qt 5 books* for Packt.

> *I would like to thank the online programming communities, bloggers, and my peers from earlier organizations, from whom I have learned a lot over the years.*

Packt is searching for authors like you

If you're interested in becoming an author for Packt, please visit `authors.packtpub.com` and apply today. We have worked with thousands of developers and tech professionals, just like you, to help them share their insight with the global tech community. You can make a general application, apply for a specific hot topic that we are recruiting an author for, or submit your own idea.

Table of Contents

Preface

There are many buzzwords in computing today, most of which revolve around various software technologies and concepts. Browsers have become the preferred means of accessing information and consuming all manner of data. But there is still a void that can only be filled by standalone applications that must be installed and run on an operating system. The browser itself as an application cannot be accessed through a browser and bears witness to this assertion.

Applications such as VLC, Adobe Photoshop, Google Earth, and QGIS are a few examples of applications that run directly on an operating system. Interestingly enough, these well-known software brands are built with Qt.

Qt (pronounced "cute") is a cross-platform application framework and widget toolkit that is used in creating graphical user interface applications that run on a number of different hardware and operating systems. The aforementioned applications were written using this same toolkit.

The main aim of this book is to introduce Qt to the reader. Through the use of simple and easy-to-understand examples, it will walk the user from one concept to the next without focusing too much on theory. The size of the book requires us to be concise in our presentation of materials. Coupled with the ample examples presented, we hope to shorten the path to understanding and learning how to use Qt.

Who this book is for

Anyone looking to embark on the development of graphical user interface applications will find this book useful. No prior exposure to other toolkits is required in order to understand this book. However, having such skills will prove useful.

The book does, however, presume that you have a working knowledge in the use of C++. If you can express your thoughts in developing algorithms and the use of object-oriented programming, you will find the content easy to consume.

Expert or intermediate persons with Qt knowledge should seek more detailed materials that are available out there. This book is not a reference guide, and should only be used as introductory material.

What this book covers

Chapter 1, *Introducing Qt 5*, walks you through the process of getting your machine ready to starting writing and running Qt programs. The chapter ends by introducing the hello world program in Qt, exploring the general structure and compilation process of a Qt program.

Chapter 2, *Creating Widgets and Layouts*, covers GUI components that are usually present in most applications and how they are created in Qt. The chapter then ends by detailing how to use layouts with widgets.

Chapter 3, *Working with Signals and Slots*, introduces one of the most important concepts to grasp in Qt, signals and slots. It demonstrates to the reader how to make an application trigger and respond to actions.

Chapter 4, *Implementing Windows and Dialog*, brings the reader closer to how a real-world Qt program should be written. It illustrates how to use and organize a program using classes, windows, and dialog boxes.

Chapter 5, *Managing Events, Custom Signals, and Slots*, explores the writing of custom signals and slots and introduces the topic of Events in Qt.

Chapter 6, *Connecting Qt with Databases*, deals with how to write applications that connect to a database and how to also present the data in visual form.

To get the most out of this book

The beginning of each chapter will begin with a little theory that should help consolidate your understanding. Thereafter, a series of examples are used to explain the concepts and to help the reader grasp the topic better.

This book also avoids continuing with examples from previous chapters. Each chapter's examples are short and do not require the reader to have knowledge of previous chapters. That way, you can pick any chapter you link and work through it.

Appropriate links to set up the environment on Windows have been provided. Linux and macOS platforms have been catered for directly in this book.

Download the example code files

You can download the example code files for this book from your account at
`www.packt.com`. If you purchased this book elsewhere, you can visit
`www.packt.com/support` and register to have the files emailed directly to you.

You can download the code files by following these steps:

1. Log in or register at `www.packt.com`.
2. Select the **SUPPORT** tab.
3. Click on **Code Downloads & Errata**.
4. Enter the name of the book in the **Search** box and follow the onscreen instructions.

Once the file is downloaded, please make sure that you unzip or extract the folder using the latest version of:

- WinRAR/7-Zip for Windows
- Zipeg/iZip/UnRarX for Mac
- 7-Zip/PeaZip for Linux

The code bundle for the book is also hosted on GitHub at `https://github.com/PacktPublishing/Getting-Started-with-Qt-5`. In case there's an update to the code, it will be updated on the existing GitHub repository.

We also have other code bundles from our rich catalog of books and videos available at `https://github.com/PacktPublishing/`. Check them out!

Download the color images

We also provide a PDF file that has color images of the screenshots/diagrams used in this book. You can download it here: `https://www.packtpub.com/sites/default/files/downloads/9781789956030_ColorImages.pdf`.

Conventions used

There are a number of text conventions used throughout this book.

`CodeInText`: Indicates code words in text, database table names, folder names, filenames, file extensions, pathnames, dummy URLs, user input, and Twitter handles. Here is an example: "To set the password to the `connection` parameter, the code fragment, `db_conn.setPassword("")`, is issued."

A block of code is set as follows:

```
QSqlDatabase db_conn =
        QSqlDatabase::addDatabase("QMYSQL", "contact_db");

db_conn.setHostName("127.0.0.1");
db_conn.setDatabaseName("contact_db");
db_conn.setUserName("root");
db_conn.setPassword("");
db_conn.setPort(3306);
```

When we wish to draw your attention to a particular part of a code block, the relevant lines or items are set in bold:

```
[default]
exten => s,1,Dial(Zap/1|30)
exten => s,2,Voicemail(u100)
exten => s,102,Voicemail(b100)
exten => i,1,Voicemail(s0)
```

Any command-line input or output is written as follows:

```
% mkdir helloWorld
% ./run_executable
```

Bold: Indicates a new term, an important word, or words that you see on screen. For example, words in menus or dialog boxes appear in the text like this. Here is an example: "It displays the text **Hello world !** in a label."

 Warnings or important notes appear like this.

Tips and tricks appear like this.

Get in touch

Feedback from our readers is always welcome.

General feedback: If you have questions about any aspect of this book, mention the book title in the subject of your message and email us at customercare@packtpub.com.

Errata: Although we have taken every care to ensure the accuracy of our content, mistakes do happen. If you have found a mistake in this book, we would be grateful if you would report this to us. Please visit www.packt.com/submit-errata, selecting your book, clicking on the Errata Submission Form link, and entering the details.

Piracy: If you come across any illegal copies of our works in any form on the internet, we would be grateful if you would provide us with the location address or website name. Please contact us at copyright@packt.com with a link to the material.

If you are interested in becoming an author: If there is a topic that you have expertise in, and you are interested in either writing or contributing to a book, please visit authors.packtpub.com.

Reviews

Please leave a review. Once you have read and used this book, why not leave a review on the site that you purchased it from? Potential readers can then see and use your unbiased opinion to make purchase decisions, we at Packt can understand what you think about our products, and our authors can see your feedback on their book. Thank you!

For more information about Packt, please visit packt.com.

Introducing Qt 5

Qt gives developers a great toolbox with which to create fantastic and practical applications with minimal stress, as you will soon discover. In this chapter, we will introduce Qt and describe how to set it up on a machine. By the end of the chapter, you should be able to do the following:

- Install Qt
- Write a simple program in Qt
- Compile and run a Qt program

The objectives have been kept simple and straightforward. So let's get started!

Installing Qt on Linux

The Ubuntu operating system makes it reasonably easy to install Qt 5. Issue the following commands to set up your box:

```
sudo apt-get install qt5-default
```

After the installation, Qt programs will be compiled and run from the command line. In Chapter 6, *Connecting Qt with Databases*, we will illustrate how to connect to the database using Qt. Issue the following command to ensure that the relevant libraries are installed for Qt to work with. The database that will'll connect to is MySQL:

```
sudo apt-get install libqt5sql5-mysql
```

Installing Qt on macOS

There are a variety of ways to get Qt installed on a Mac. To begin the process of installing Qt 5 on your Mac, you need to get Xcode installed on your machine. Issue the following commands on the Terminal:

```
xcode-select --install
```

If you get the following output, then you are ready for the next series of steps:

```
xcode-select: error: command line tools are already installed, use
"Software Update" to install updates
```

HomeBrew is a package management software tool that allows you to easily install Unix tools that don't come shipped with the macOS.

If you don't already have it on your machine, you can install it by issuing the following command in a Terminal:

```
/user/bin/ruby -e "$(curl -fsSL https://raw.githubusercontent.com/
Homebrew/install/master/install)"
```

After that, you should issue yet another set of commands to get Qt installed via the Terminal:

```
curl -O
https://raw.githubusercontent.com/Homebrew/homebrew-core/fdfc724dd532345f5c
6cdf47dc43e99654e6a5fd/Formula/qt5.rb

brew install ./qt5.rb
```

In a few chapters' time, we will be working with the MySql database. To configure Qt 5 with MySql, issue the following command:

```
brew install ./qt5 --with-mysql
```

This command should take a while to complete and, assuming nothing goes wrong, you are ready to write Qt programs.

Installation on Windows

For readers using Windows, installation remains simple, albeit a little less straightforward. We can start by heading over to http://download.qt.io.

Select `official_releases/`, then `online_installers/`, and opt to download `qt-unified-windows-x86-online.exe`.

Run the program and opt to create an account. Click through to select the installation folder and don't forget to select the **MinGW 5.3.0 32 bit** option as the compiler when selecting the components that need to be installed.

Most of the commands in this book should run in this IDE.

What is Qt?

Now that we have set up our boxes to start development, let's put together a hello world example. First, however, let's take a brief detour.

Qt is a toolkit for creating **Graphical User Interfaces** (**GUI**), as well as cross-platform applications. GUI applications are programs that employ the use of the mouse to issue commands to the computer for execution. Though Qt can, in some cases, be used without necessarily making use of this, therein lies its utility.

The difficulty in trying to produce the same look, feel, and functionality across multiple operating systems is one big hurdle you have to deal with when writing GUI applications. Qt completely does away with this impediment by providing a means to write code only once and ensuring that it runs on most operating systems without requiring much or any change.

Qt makes use of some modules. These modules group related functionalities together. The following lists some modules and what they do:

- `QtCore`: As the name implies, these modules contains core and important classes for the Qt framework. These include containers, events, and thread management, among others.
- `QtWidgets` and `QtGui`: This module contains classes for calling widgets. Widgets are the components that make up the majority of a graphical interface. These include buttons, textboxes, and labels.
- `QtWebkit`: This module makes it possible to use web pages and apps within a Qt application.
- `QtNetwork`: This module provides classes to connect to and communicate with network resources.

- QtXML: For parsing XML documents, this module contains useful classes.
- QtSQL: This module is feature-rich with classes and drivers that allow for connecting to databases, including My SQL, PostgreSQL, and SQLite.

Hello world in Qt

In this section, we will put together a very simple hello world program. The program will show a simple button within a window. Create a file called hello.cpp in a newly created folder called hello_world. Open the file and insert the code:

```cpp
#include <QApplication>
#include <QLabel>
int main(int argc, char *argv[])
{
    QApplication app(argc, argv);
    QLabel label("Hello world !");
    label.show();
    return app.exec();
}
```

This looks like a regular C++ program, with the exception of unfamiliar classes being used.

Like any regular program, the int main() function is the entry point of our application.

An instance of the QApplication class is created, called app, and the arguments passed to the main() function. The app object is required because it sets off the Event loop that continues to run until we close the application. Without the QApplication object, you cannot really create a Qt GUI application.

 However, it is possible to use certain aspects of Qt without the need to create an instance of QApplication.

Also, the constructor for QApplication requires that we pass the argc and argv to it.

We instantiate an object of the QLabel class, label. We pass the "Hello World!" string to its constructor. A QLabel represents what we call a widget, which is a term used to describe visual elements on the screen. Labels are used to hold text for display.

By default, created widgets are hidden. To display them, a call to the show() function has to be made.

To start the Event loop, the app.exec() line is executed. This passes control of the application to Qt.

The return keyword will pass an integer back to the operating system, indicating the state of the application when it was closed or exited.

To compile and run our program, navigate to the folder where hello.cpp is stored. Type the following command in the Terminal:

```
% qmake -project
```

This will create the hello_world.pro file. The name hello_world is the name of the folder where hello.cpp is located. The generated file should change, depending on the location you stored the hello.cpp file.

Open the hello_world.pro file with any text editor of your choice. The following lines deserve some explanation:

```
TEMPLATE = app
```

The value, app, here means that the final output of the project will be an application. Alternatively, it could be a library or sub-directory:

```
TARGET = hello_world
```

The name, hello_world, here is the name of the application or (library) that will be executed:

```
SOURCES += hello.cpp
```

Since hello.cpp is the only source file in our project, it is added to the SOURCES variable.

We need to generate a Makefile that will detail the steps needed to compile our hello world program. The benefit of this autogenerated Makefile is that it takes away the need for us to know the various nuances involved in compiling the program on the different operating systems.

While in the same project directory, issue the following command:

```
% qmake
```

This generates a Makefile in the directory.

Now, issue the following command to compile the program:

```
% make
```

The following error will be produced (along with further information) as the output from running the `make` command:

```
#include <QApplication>
         ^~~~~~~~~~~~
```

Earlier on, we mentioned that various components and classes are packaged into modules. The `QApplication` is being utilized in our application, but the correct module has not been included. During compilation, this omission results in an error.

To fix this issue, open the `hello_world.pro` file and insert the following lines after the line:

```
INCLUDEPATH += .
QT += widgets
```

This will add the `QtWidget` module, along with the `QtCore` modules, to the compiled program. With the correct module added, run the `make` command again on the command line:

```
% make
```

A `hello_world` file will be generated in the same folder. Run this file from the command line as follows:

```
% ./hello_world
```

On a macOS, the full path to the executable will be specified with the following path from the command line:

```
./hello_world.app/Contents/MacOS/hello_world
```

This should produce the following output:

Well, there is our first GUI program. It displays the **Hello world !** in a label. To close the application, click on the **Close** button of the window.

Let's add a dash of **Qt Style Sheet** (**QSS**) to give our label a little effect!

Modify the `hello.cpp` file as follows:

```
#include <QApplication>
#include <QLabel>
int main(int argc, char *argv[])
{
    QApplication app(argc, argv);
    QLabel label("Hello world !");
    label.setStyleSheet("QLabel:hover { color: rgb(60, 179, 113)}");
    label.show();
    return app.exec();
}
```

The only change here is `label.setStyleSheet("QLabel:hover { color: rgb(60, 179, 113)}");`.

A QSS rule is passed as an argument to the `setStyleSheet` method on the `label` object. The rule sets every label within our application to show the color green when the cursor hovers over it.

Run the following commands to recompile the application and run it:

```
% make
% ./hello_world
```

The program should appear as in the following screenshot. The label turns green when the mouse is placed over it:

Summary

This chapter laid the foundation for getting to know Qt and what it can be used for. Installing of Qt on macOS and Linux was outlined. A small hello world application was written and compiled, all from the command line, without any need for an IDE. This meant that we were also introduced to the various steps that lead to the final program.

Finally, the hello world application was modified to employ QSS in a bid to show what other things can be done to a widget.

In Chapter 2, *Creating Widgets and Layouts*, we will explore more widgets in Qt and how to organize and group them.

2
Creating Widgets and Layouts

In this chapter, we shall take a look at what widgets are and the various kinds that are available for creating GUIs. For most GUI applications that you will write, Qt is laden with sufficient widgets to implement it. Coupled with widgets are layout classes, which help us to arrange and position the widgets for better appeal.

By the end of this chapter, you should be aware of the following:

- Understand and know how to use widgets
- Know the classes needed to lay out widgets

Widgets

Widgets are the graphical components with which we construct user interfaces. A familiar example of such a component is a textbox. This is the component that is used to capture our email address or last and first names on forms in a GUI application.

There are a few critical points to note regarding widgets in Qt:

- Information is passed to widgets by way of events. For a textbox, an example of an event could be when a user clicks within the textbox or when the `return` key has been pressed while a textbox cursor is blinking.
- Every widget can have a parent widget or children widgets.
- Widgets that do not have a parent widget become a window when the `show()` function is called on them. Such a widget will be enclosed in a window with buttons to close, maximize, and minimize it.
- A child widget is displayed within its parent widget.

Qt organizes its classes with heavy use of inheritance, and it is very important to have a good grasp of this. Consider the following diagram:

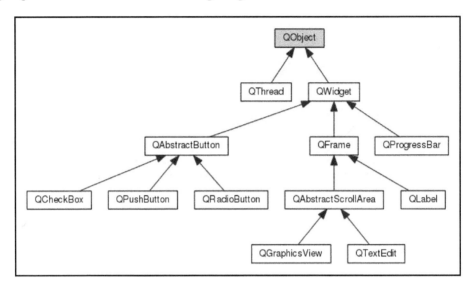

At the very top of the hierarchy is the **QObject**. A lot of classes inherit from the **QObject** class. The **QObject** class also contains the mechanisms of signals and slots and event management, among other things.

Furthermore, widgets that share common behavior are grouped together. **QCheckBox**, **QPushButton**, and **QRadioButton** are all buttons of the same kind and thus inherit from **QAbstractButton**, which holds properties and functions that are shared by all buttons. This principle also applies to **QAbstractScrollArea** and its children, **QGraphicsView** and **QTextEdit**.

To put into practice some of what we have just learned, let's create a simple Qt program with only one widget.

This Qt application displays only one button. Open a text file and name it how you want with the suffix .cpp.

Most of the examples will require that you create a new folder where the source code will be stored. This will allow for easy compilation of the program as a project.

Insert the following lines of codes. Create a new folder and move the .cpp file into it:

```
#include <QApplication>
#include <QPushButton>
int main(int argc, char *argv[])
{
    QApplication app(argc, argv);
    QPushButton myButton(QIcon("filesaveas.png"),"Push Me");
    myButton.setToolTip("Click this to turn back the hands of time");
    myButton.show();
    return app.exec();
}
```

The purpose of this application is to show how a widget without a parent object becomes the main window when executed. The button that will be created will include an icon and a tooltip.

For starters, this application looks similar to the one we wrote at the tail end of Chapter 1, *Introducing Qt 5*. In this application, a button named myButton is declared. An instance of QIcon is passed as the first argument to the default constructor of QPushButton. This reads the file named filesaveas.png (which, for now, should be in the same folder as the source code file on GitHub). The text "Push Me" is passed as the second argument. This text will be displayed on the button.

The next line, myButton.setToolTip("Click this to turn back the hands of time");, is used to set a tooltip on the button. A tooltip is a piece of text or a message that is displayed when you rest the mouse cursor over a widget. It usually holds extra or explanatory information over and above what the widget might be displaying.

Lastly, we call the show() function on the myButton object to unhide it and draw it to the screen. In this application, we only have one widget, QPushButton. What could be the parent of this widget? Well, if unspecified, the parent defaults to NULL, which tells Qt that the widget is without a parent. When displaying such a widget, it will be enclosed in a window on account of this reasoning.

Save the file and run the following commands to compile your application. Change directory to the new folder you created that houses the .cpp file created:

 The commands that should be run in a Terminal or on the command line begin with a % sign, which represents the prompt on the Terminal. Depending on the setup of your Terminal, this might be slightly different, but the command is all the characters after the % sign.

```
% qmake -project
```

From the name of the `.pro` file, it tells us that the name of the folder where the `.cpp` file is located is called `qbutton`. This name should, therefore, change to whichever folder name the `.cpp` file is located in when you issue the preceding command.

Now, remember to add the following line to the `qbutton.pro` beneath `INCLUDEPATH +=` `.:`

```
QT += widgets
```

Continue with the following commands:

```
% qmake
% make
```

Run the application from the command line according to an issue:

```
% ./qbutton
```

You should obtain the following screenshot:

The preceding screenshot shows what you will see when the program is run for the first time:

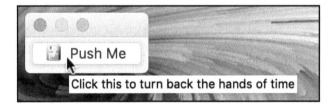

The tooltip that was specified within the code is displayed when we rest our cursor on the button, as seen in the preceding screenshot.

The button also shows the image for those cases when you want to add an image to a button in order to improve the intuitiveness of a UI.

A few observations worthy of note are the following:

- The `setToolTip()` function is not found in the `QPushButton` class. Instead, it is one of the functions that belongs to the `QWidget` class.
- This highlights the usefulness that classes get by means of inheritance.
- The property or member of the `QWiget` class that stores the value of the tooltip is `toolTip`.

To cap off this section on widgets, let's customize a `QLabel` and display it. This time, an instance of `QLabel` will have its font changed and shall display a longer text than usual.

Create a file named `qlabel_long_text.cpp` in a newly created folder and insert the following code:

```
#include <QApplication>
#include <QString>
#include <QLabel>
int main(int argc, char *argv[])
{
        QApplication app(argc, argv);
        QString message = "'What do you know about this business?' the
King said to Alice.\n'Nothing,' said Alice.\n'Nothing whatever?' persisted
the King.\n'Nothing whatever,' said Alice.";
        QLabel label(message);
        label.setFont(QFont("Comic Sans MS", 18));
        label.setAlignment(Qt::AlignCenter);
        label.show();
        return app.exec();
}
```

The structure of our Qt programs has not changed that much. The first three (3) lines have the `include` directives adding the headers for the classes we will be using.

As usual, the arguments to the `main()` function are passed to `app()`. The `message` variable is a `QString` object that holds a long string. `QString` is the class used when working with strings. It has a host of functionalities not available in C++ string.

An instance of `QLabel` is created, `label`, and `message` is passed to this. To change the style by which the label string is displayed, we pass an instance of `QFont` to the `setFont` function. We select the font style *Comic Sans MS*, with a point size of *18*, to the constructor of `QFont`.

To align all the text in the middle, we call the `setAlignment` function on the `label` object and pass the `Qt::AlignCenter` constant.

Lastly, we display the widget by calling the `show` function on the `label` object.

As usual, we shall issue the following codes on the command line to compile and run this program:

```
% qmake -project
% qmake
% ./qlabel_long_text
```

 Remember to add `QT += widgets` to the `.pro` file.

The output of the program appears as follows. All the text on the lines are centered in the middle:

'What do you know about this business?' the King said to Alice.
'Nothing,' said Alice.
'Nothing whatever?' persisted the King.
'Nothing whatever,' said Alice.

Once again, the only widget within the `label` application becomes the main window because it has no parent object associated with it. Secondly, the widget becomes a window because the `show()` method was called on `label`.

Layouts

Up to this point, we have been creating applications that only have one widget serving as the main component and, by extension, a window too. However, GUI applications are usually made up of several widgets that come together to communicate a process to the user. One way in which we can make use of multiple widgets is to use layouts to serve as the canvas into which we insert our widgets.

Consider the following class inheritance diagram:

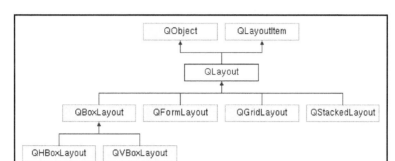

It is important to consider the classes used in laying out widgets. As usual, the top class from which the QLayout abstract class inherits is QObject. Also, QLayout makes use of multiple inheritances by inheriting from QLayoutItem. The concrete classes here are QBoxLayout, QFormLayout, QGridLayout, and QStackedLayout. QHBoxLayout and QVBoxLayout further refine what the QBoxLayout class is by adding orientation to how the widgets within a layout might be arranged.

The following table provides a brief description of what the major layouts do:

Layout class	Description
QFormLayout	The QFormLayout class (https://doc.qt.io/qt-5/qformlayout.html) manages forms of input widgets and their associated labels.
QGridLayout	The QGridLayout class (https://doc.qt.io/qt-5/qgridlayout.html) lays out widgets in a grid.
QStackedLayout	The QStackedLayout class (https://doc.qt.io/qt-5/qstackedlayout.html) provides a stack of widgets where only one widget is visible at a time.
QVBoxLayout	The QVBoxLayout class (https://doc.qt.io/qt-5/qvboxlayout.html) lines up widgets vertically.
QHBoxLayout	The QHBoxLayout class (https://doc.qt.io/qt-5/qhboxlayout.html) lines up widgets horizontally.

We need to lay out the widgets for two main reasons:

- To allow us to display more than one widget.
- To present the many widgets in our interface nicely and intuitively to allow the UI to be useful. Not all GUIs allows users to do their work well. Bad layout can confuse the users of a system and make them struggle to use it properly.

Let's create a simple program to illustrate how to use some of the layout classes.

QGridLayout

The QGridLayout is used to arrange widgets by specifying the number of rows and columns that will be filled up by multiple widgets. A grid-like structure mimics a table in that it has rows and columns and widgets are inserted as cells where a row and column meet.

Create a new folder and, using of any editor, create a file named main.cpp:

```cpp
#include <QApplication>
#include <QPushButton>
#include <QGridLayout>
#include <QLineEdit>
#include <QDateTimeEdit>
#include <QSpinBox>
#include <QComboBox>
#include <QLabel>
#include <QStringList>
int main(int argc, char *argv[])
{
    QApplication app(argc, argv);
    QWidget *window = new QWidget;
    QLabel *nameLabel = new QLabel("Open Happiness");
    QLineEdit *firstNameLineEdit= new QLineEdit;
    QLineEdit *lastNameLineEdit= new QLineEdit;
    QSpinBox *ageSpinBox = new QSpinBox;
    ageSpinBox->setRange(1, 100);
    QComboBox *employmentStatusComboBox= new QComboBox;
    QStringList employmentStatus = {"Unemployed", "Employed", "NA"};
    employmentStatusComboBox->addItems(employmentStatus);
    QGridLayout *layout = new QGridLayout;
    layout->addWidget(nameLabel, 0, 0);
    layout->addWidget(firstNameLineEdit, 0, 1);
    layout->addWidget(lastNameLineEdit, 0, 2);
    layout->addWidget(ageSpinBox, 1, 0);
    layout->addWidget(employmentStatusComboBox, 1, 1,1,2);
    window->setLayout(layout);
    window->show();
    return app.exec();
}
```

The aim of the program is to illustrate how to use a layout object. To fill up the layout, other widgets will be discussed too.

In the preceding code, `*window` is an instance of `QWidget`. For now, keep this object in to see and how we shall turn it into a window.

The widgets that we are going to insert into our layout are created thereafter, namely `name`, `firstnameLineEdit`, and `lastNameLineEdit`.

 Some prefer to name their variables by appending the name of the class that they are instantiating to it. The CamelCase naming scheme is being used here too.

`QLineEdit` is essentially the class for creating textboxes. `QSpinbox` is a widget that allows for the selection of a value between a given range. In this case, `ageSpinBox->setRange(1, 100)` sets the range of possible values between `1` and `100`.

Next, we instantiate the `QComboBox` class to create a widget with drop-down values specified by a list of strings stored in `QStringList`. The list of strings, `employmentStatus`, is then passed to `employmentStatusComboBox` by calling its `addItems()` method. These will become the options that will be displayed when the widget is clicked.

Since we want to layout our widgets in a grid layout, we create an object from the `QGridLayout`, `*layout`. To add the widgets to the layout, the `addWIdget()` method is called and each time, the widget, along with two (2) numbers that specify the row and column where the widget is to be inserted is specified:

```
layout->addWidget(nameLabel, 0, 0);
layout->addWidget(firstNameLineEdit, 0, 1);
layout->addWidget(lastNameLineEdit, 0, 2);
layout->addWidget(ageSpinBox, 1, 0);
layout->addWidget(employmentStatusComboBox, 1, 1,1,2);
```

The first widget to be inserted into the layout object is the label, `nameLabel`. This occupies the first row and first column of the grid. The first row is represented by the second parameter `0` while the first column is represented by `0`. This resolves to the selection of the first cell of the grid to keep `nameLabel`.

The second widget that is added to the layout is `firstNameLineEdit`. This widget will be inserted on the first row, marked by `0`, and on the second column marked by `1`. Next to this widget is added the `lastNameLineEdit` widget, also sitting on the same row, `0`.

The `ageSpinBox` widget will be fixed on the second row marked by `1` and in the first column, marked by `0`.

The `employmentStatusComboBox` widget is added to the `layout` object and further stretches out by specifying the `rowspan` with the last `(1, 2)` arguments that are passed along:

```
window->setLayout(layout);
window->show();
```

The `window` object is without a layout. To set the layout of the widget, call `setLayout` and pass in the layout object, which holds the other widgets.

Because `window`, which is basically a widget, has no parent object, it will become a window when we call the `show()` method on it. Also, all the widgets that were added to the layout object via the `addWidget()` method are children of the `layout` object.

Run the project by issuing the commands to create the project and compiling on the command line.

You should see this on successful compilation:

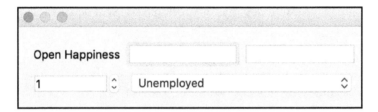

Notice how the drop-down widget stretches to fill the third column. The placement of the widgets conforms to how we laid out the widgets as we called `addWidget()`. Experiment by clicking on the `ageSpinBox` to observe how it behaves.

In the next section, we shall take a look at a useful layout class called `QFormLayout`.

QFormLayout

For those instances when you simply need to place a number of widgets together in a two-column layout, the `QFormLayout` is useful. You may choose to construct a form using `QGridLayout`, but for form presentation, `QFormLayout` is most suited.

Take, for instance, the following code. It illustrates a form that has labels in the first column and the actual control for taking user input in the second column:

```
#include <QApplication>
#include <QFormLayout>
#include <QPushButton>
#include <QLineEdit>
#include <QSpinBox>
#include <QComboBox>
#include <QStringList>
int main(int argc, char *argv[])
{
    QApplication app(argc, argv);
    QWidget *window = new QWidget;
    QLineEdit *firstNameLineEdit= new QLineEdit;
    QLineEdit *lastNameLineEdit= new QLineEdit;
    QSpinBox *ageSpingBox = new QSpinBox;
    QComboBox *employmentStatusComboBox= new QComboBox;
    QStringList employmentStatus = {"Unemployed", "Employed", "NA"};
    ageSpingBox->setRange(1, 100);
    employmentStatusComboBox->addItems(employmentStatus);
    QFormLayout *personalInfoformLayout = new QFormLayout;
    personalInfoformLayout->addRow("First Name:", firstNameLineEdit);
    personalInfoformLayout->addRow("Last Name:", lastNameLineEdit );
    personalInfoformLayout->addRow("Age", ageSpingBox);
    personalInfoformLayout->addRow("Employment Status",
    employmentStatusComboBox);
    window->setLayout(personalInfoformLayout);
    window->show();
    return app.exec();
}
```

The code should look familiar by now. We instantiate objects of the various widgets we want to show in the form. Thereafter, the layout is created:

```
QFormLayout *personalInfoformLayout = new QFormLayout;
```

An instance of `QFormLayout` is created. Anytime we want to add a widget to the layout, `*personalInformformLayout`, we shall call the `addRow()` method, pass a string representing the label and finally the widget we want to align with the label:

```
personalInfoformLayout->addRow("First Name:", firstNameLineEdit);
```

`"First Name: "` is the label and the widget here is `firstNameLineEdit`.

The other widgets are added to the layout like this:

```
window->setLayout(personalInfoformLayout);
```

personalInfoformLayout is then passed to the setLayout() method of the QWidget instance. This means that the layout for the application window, window, is personalInfoformLayout.

Remember that the QWidget instance, window, will become the main window of the application since its show() method is called.

QForm eliminates the need to specify columns and rows by giving us an easy way to add a row to our layout, and each time we do so, we can specify the label and the widget we want displayed.

You should see this output when you compile and run the project:

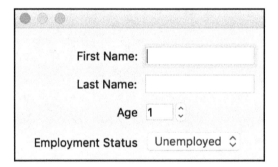

The preceding screenshot shows how widgets are aligned in those layouts. A form is presented in a question-and-answer manner. The labels are usually on the left-hand side while the widgets that take the user input are on the right-hand side.

Layouts with direction

There are layouts that provide direction of growth when widgets are added to them. There are instances where we want to align all widgets within a layout horizontally or vertically.

The QHBoxLayout and QVBoxLayout classes provide this functionality.

QVBoxLayout

In a `QVBoxLayout` layout, widgets are aligned vertically and they are packed in the layout from top to bottom.

Consider the following diagram:

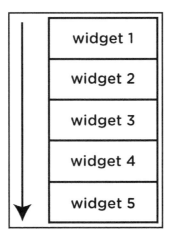

For `QVBoxLayout`, the arrow gives the direction of growth in which the widgets are added to the layout. The first widget, **widget 1**, will occupy the top of the layout, while the last call to `addWidget()` will make **widget 5** occupy the bottom of the layout.

To illustrate how to use the `QVBoxLayout`, consider the following program:

```cpp
#include <QApplication>
#include <QVBoxLayout>
#include <QPushButton>
#include <QLabel>
#include <QLineEdit>
int main(int argc, char *argv[])
{
    QApplication app(argc, argv);
    QWidget *window = new QWidget;
    QLabel *label1 = new QLabel("Username");
    QLabel *label2 = new QLabel("Password");
    QLineEdit *usernameLineEdit = new QLineEdit;
    usernameLineEdit->setPlaceholderText("Enter your username");
    QLineEdit *passwordLineEdit = new QLineEdit;
    passwordLineEdit->setEchoMode(QLineEdit::Password);
    passwordLineEdit->setPlaceholderText("Enter your password");
    QPushButton *button1 = new QPushButton("&Login");
```

```
        QPushButton *button2 = new QPushButton("&Register");
        QVBoxLayout *layout = new QVBoxLayout;
        layout->addWidget(label1);
        layout->addWidget(usernameLineEdit);
        layout->addWidget(label2);
        layout->addWidget(passwordLineEdit);
        layout->addWidget(button1);
        layout->addWidget(button2);
        window->setLayout(layout);
        window->show();
        return app.exec();
    }
```

In previous examples, we indicated the reason why we create an instance of `QWidget`. Two labels are created with the strings `"Username"` and `"Password"`. A textbox, `QLineEdit` instance is also created to receive both username and password input. On the `passwordLineEdit` object, the `setEchoMode()` method is passed the constant `QLineEdit::Password` that masks the input of that textbox and replaces it with dots to prevent the characters that are typed from being readable.

A placeholder text within `passwordLineEdit` is set via the `setPlaceholderText()` method. The placeholder text gives further information about the purpose of the textbox.

Two push buttons are also created, `button1` and `button2`. An instance of `QVBoxLayout` is created. To add widgets to the layout, the `addWidget()` method is called and passed the specific widget. The very first widget passed to `addWidget` will appear on top when displayed. Likewise, the last widget added will show on the bottom, which in this case is `button2`.

The layout for the `window` widget instance is set by passing `layout` to `setLayout()`.

Finally, the `show()` method is called on the window. Compile the project and run it to see the output:

In the preceding screenshot, we can see that the first widget that was added to the layout was the label, label1, while button2 (with the text **Register**) was the last widget occupying the bottom.

QHBoxLayout

The QHBoxLayout layout class is very similar in use to QVBoxLayout. Widgets are added to the layout by calling the addWidget() method.

Consider the following diagram:

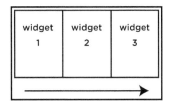

The arrow in the diagram shows the direction in which widgets grow in number as they are added to a QHBoxLayout. The first widget added to this layout is **widget 1**, while **widget 3** is the last widget to be added to the layout.

A small application to allow users to enter a URL makes use of this layout type:

```
#include <QApplication>
#include <QHBoxLayout>
#include <QPushButton>
#include <QLineEdit>
int main(int argc, char *argv[])
{
    QApplication app(argc, argv);
    QWidget *window = new QWidget;
    QLineEdit *urlLineEdit= new QLineEdit;
    QPushButton *exportButton = new QPushButton("Export");
    urlLineEdit->setPlaceholderText("Enter Url to export. Eg,
http://yourdomain.com/items");
    urlLineEdit->setFixedWidth(400);
    QHBoxLayout *layout = new QHBoxLayout;
    layout->addWidget(urlLineEdit);
    layout->addWidget(exportButton);
    window->setLayout(layout);
    window->show();
    return app.exec();
}
```

A textbox or QLineEdit and button are created. A placeholder is set on the QLineEdit instance, urlLineEdit. To enable the placeholder to be seen, we stretch urlLineEdit by setting setFixedWidth to 400.

An instance of QHBoxLayout is created and passed to the layout pointer. The two widgets, urlLineEdit and exportButton, are added to the layout via the addWidget() method.

The layout is set against window and the show() method of the window is called.

Compile the application and run it. You should see the following output:

Refer to Chapter 1, *Introducing Qt 5*, to compile the application. For easy compilation process, remember to create a new folder and add the .cpp file to it. As usual, the .pro file will need to be changed to include the widgets module.

Because the button was added to the layout after textbox, it appears accordingly, standing next to the textbox. If another widget had been added to the layout, it would also appear after the button, exportButton.

Summary

In this chapter, we have looked at a number of widgets that are useful in creating GUI applications. The process of compilation remains the same. We also learned how to use layouts to present and arrange multiple widgets.

Up to this point, our application does not do anything. The QPushButton instances, when clicked, do nothing along with the other widgets that are action driven.

In the next chapter, we shall learn how to animate our application so that it responds to actions, thus making them useful.

Working with Signals and Slots 3

Thus far, we have learned how to create applications and display various kinds of widgets. If that were all that GUI applications were made of, that would be the end of the matter. But there is more that we need to do in order to make our applications usable. In this chapter, we will set about the following:

- Understanding the concept behind signals and slots
- Learning the different ways to connect signals and slots

GUI toolkits usually provide a means to react to things that occur within an application. Nothing is left to chance. Every tick that happens within the application is registered and taken note of. For example, when you move a window or resize it, the action gets registered, and provided ample code has been written, it will be executed as a reaction to the moving or resizing of the window. For every action that occurs, a number of outcomes may happen. Essentially, the questions we want to answer are as follows: what do we do when a particular action or event has occurred? How do we handle it?

One way to implement the ability to react to an action that has occurred is by using the design pattern called the **Observer Pattern**.

In the Observer Pattern design, an observable object communicates its state change to other objects that are observing it. For instance, any time an object (A) wants to be notified of a state change of some other object (B), it first has to identify that object (B) and register itself as one of the objects that should receive such notification of the state change. Sometime in the future, when the state of an object (B) occurs, object (B) will go through a list of objects it keeps that want to be informed regarding the state change. This will, at this point, include object (A):

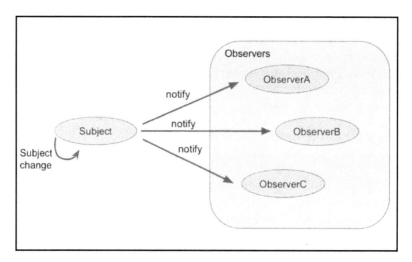

From the preceding diagram, the **Subject** circle is termed the observable object, while the circles in the bounded box are the observers. They are being notified of the state change of the **Subject** as its count variable is increased from 1 to 5.

Some events or actions that may occur within our application that we will be interested in and would want to react to include the following:

- A window being resized
- A button clicked
- Pressing the return key
- A widget being dragged
- A mouse hovering over the widget

In the case of a button, a typical response to a click of a mouse would be to start a download process or send an email.

Signals and slots

In Qt, this action-response scheme is handled by signals and slots. This section will include a few definitions, and then we shall jump into an example for further explanation.

A signal is a message that is passed to communicate that the state of an object has changed. This signal may carry information about the change that has occurred. For instance, when a window has been resized, the signal will usually carry the coordinates of the new state (or size) of the window. Sometimes, a signal may carry no extra information, such as that of a button click.

A slot is a specific function of an object that is called whenever a certain signal has been emitted. Since slots are functions, they will embody lines of code that perform an action, such as closing a window, disabling a button, and sending an email, to mention but a few.

Signals and slots have to be connected (in code). Without writing code to connect a signal and a slot, they will exist as independent entities.

Most of the widgets in Qt come with a number of signals and slots. However, it is possible to write your own signals and slots too.

So what do a signal and a slot look like?

Consider the following code listing:

```cpp
#include <QApplication>
#include <QPushButton>
int main(int argc, char *argv[])
{
    QApplication app(argc, argv);
    QPushButton *quitButton = new QPushButton("Quit");
    QObject::connect(quitButton, SIGNAL(clicked()),
            &app, SLOT(quit()));
    quitButton->show();
    return app.exec();
}
```

As usual, we shall use the following steps to compile the project:

1. Create a new folder with an appropriate name of your choosing
2. Create a .cpp file named main.cpp

3. Issue the following commands in the Terminal:

```
% qmake -project
% qmake
% make
% ./executable_file
```

Be sure to edit the .pro file to include the widget module during compilation.

Compile and run the application.

An instance of QPushButton is created, quitButton. The quitButton instance here is the observable object. Anytime this button is clicked, the clicked() signal will be emitted. The clicked() signal here is a method belonging to the QPushButton class that has only been earmarked as a signal.

The quit() method of the app object is called, which terminates the event loop.

To specify what should happen when quitButton has been clicked, we pass app and say that the quit() method on the app object should be called. These four parameters are connected by the static function, connect(), of the QObject class.

The general format is (objectA, *signals* (methodOnObjectA()), objectB, *slots* (methodOnObjectB())).

The second and final parameters are the signatures of the methods representing the signals and the slots. The first and third parameters are pointers and should contain the address to objects. Since quitButton is already a pointer, we simply pass it as it is. On the other hand, &app would return the address of app.

Now, click on the button and the application will close:

When this application is run, you should see the following.

The example we have just illustrated is quite primitive. Let's write an application where a change in the state of one widget is passed to another widget. Not only will the signal be connected to a slot, but data will be carried along:

```
#include <QApplication>
#include <QVBoxLayout>
#include <QLabel>
#include <QDial>
int main(int argc, char *argv[])
{
    QApplication app(argc, argv);
    QWidget *window = new QWidget;
    QVBoxLayout *layout = new QVBoxLayout;
    QLabel *volumeLabel = new QLabel("0");
    QDial *volumeDial= new QDial;
    layout->addWidget(volumeDial);
    layout->addWidget(volumeLabel);
    QObject::connect(volumeDial, SIGNAL(valueChanged(int)), volumeLabel,
    SLOT(setNum(int)));
    window->setLayout(layout);
    window->show();
    return app.exec();
}
```

This is yet another simple program that illustrates how data is passed between the signal and slot. An instance of `QVBoxLayout` is created, `layout`. A `QLabel` instance, `volumeLabel`, is created and will be used to display changes that occur. It is initialized with the string 0. Next, an instance of `QDial` is created with `QDial *volumeDial = new QDial`. The `QDial` widget is a knob-like looking widget that is graduated with a minimum and maximum range of numbers. With the aid of a mouse, the knob can be turned, just like you would turn up the volume on a speaker or radio.

These two widgets, `volumeLabel` and `volumeDial`, are then added to the layout using the `addWidget()` method.

Whenever we change to move the knob of `QDial`, a signal called `valueChanged(int)` is emitted. The slot named `setNum(int)` of the `volumeLabel` object is a method that accepts an `int` value.

Note how the connection between the signals and slots is established in the following code:

```
QObject::connect(volumeDial, SIGNAL(valueChanged(int)), volumeLabel,
SLOT(setNum(int)));
```

This literally establishes a connection that reads "*Anytime the* QDial *changes its value, call the* setNum() *method of the* volumeLabel *object and pass it an* int *value.*" There can be a number of state changes that may occur in QDial. The connection further makes it explicit that we are only interested in the value that has changed when the knob (QDial) was moved, which, in turn, emitted its current value through the valueChanged(int) signal.

To dry run the program, let's assume that the range of QDial is representing a radio volume range between 0 and 100. If the knob of QDial is changed to half of the range, the valueChanged(50) signal will be emitted. Now, the value 50 will be passed to the setNum(50) function. This will be used to set the text of the label, volumeLabel in our example, to display **50**.

Compile the application and run it. The following output will be displayed on the first run:

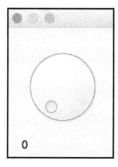

As you can see, the initial state of QDial is zero. The following label shows that too. Move the dial, and you will see that the label will have its value change accordingly. The following screenshot shows the state of the application after the knob has been moved to half of the range:

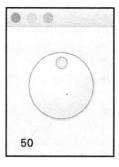

Move the knob around and observe how the label changes accordingly. This is all made possible by means of the signals and slots mechanism.

Signals and slots configuration

It is not only possible to connect one signal to one slot, but to connect one signal to more than one slot. This involves repeating the `QObject::connect()` call and, in each instance, specifying the slot that should be called when a particular signal has been emitted.

Single signal, multiple slots

In this section, we shall concern ourselves with how to connect a single signal to multiple slots.

Examine the following program:

```cpp
#include <QApplication>
#include <QVBoxLayout>
#include <QLabel>
#include <QDial>
#include <QLCDNumber>
int main(int argc, char *argv[])
{
    QApplication app(argc, argv);
    QWidget *window = new QWidget;
    QVBoxLayout *layout = new QVBoxLayout;
    QLabel *volumeLabel = new QLabel("0");
    QDial *volumeDial= new QDial;
    QLCDNumber *volumeLCD = new QLCDNumber;
    volumeLCD->setPalette(Qt::red);
    volumeLabel->setAlignment(Qt::AlignHCenter);
    volumeDial->setNotchesVisible(true);
    volumeDial->setMinimum(0);
    volumeDial->setMaximum(100);
    layout->addWidget(volumeDial);
    layout->addWidget(volumeLabel);
    layout->addWidget(volumeLCD);
    QObject::connect(volumeDial, SIGNAL(valueChanged(int)), volumeLabel,
    SLOT(setNum(int)));
    QObject::connect(volumeDial, SIGNAL(valueChanged(int)), volumeLCD ,
    SLOT(display(int)));
    window->setLayout(layout);
    window->show();
    return app.exec();
}
```

We want to illustrate how one signal can be connected to two different slots, or more than one slot for that matter. The widget that will be emitting the signal is an instance of `QDial`, `volumeDial`. An instance of `QLCDNumber`, `volumeLCD` is created. This widget displays information in an LCD-like digit form. Note `volumeLabel` is an instance of a `QLabel`. These two widgets shall provide the two slots.

To make the text of `volumeLCD` stand out, we set the color of the display to red with `volumeLCD->setPalette(Qt::red);`.

The fact that `layout` is an instance of `QVBoxLayout` means that widgets added to this layout will flow from top to bottom. Each widget added to the layout will be centered around the middle as we set `setAlignment(Qt::AlignHCenter);` on `volumeLabel`:

```
volumeDial->setNotchesVisible(true);
volumeDial->setMinimum(0);
volumeDial->setMaximum(100);
```

The graduations on `volumeDial` are visible when the `setNotchesVisible(true)` method is called. The default argument to `setNotchesVisible()` is `false`, which makes the small ticks (graduations) on the dial invisible. The range for our `QDial` instance is set by calling `setMinimum(0)` and `setMaximum(100)`.

The three widgets are added accordingly with each call to the `addWidget()` method:

```
layout->addWidget(volumeDial);
layout->addWidget(volumeLabel);
layout->addWidget(volumeLCD);
```

Now, `volumeDial` emits the signal, `valueChanged(int)`, which we connect to the `setNum(int)` slot of `volumeLabel`. When the knob of `volumeDial` changes, the current value will be sent for display in `volumeLabel`:

```
QObject::connect(volumeDial, SIGNAL(valueChanged(int)), volumeLabel,
SLOT(setNum(int)));
QObject::connect(volumeDial, SIGNAL(valueChanged(int)), volumeLCD ,
SLOT(display(int)));
```

This same signal, `valueChanged(int)` of `volumeDial`, is also connected to the `display(int)` slot of `volumeLCD`.

The total effect of these two connections is that when there is a change in `volumeDial`, both `volumeLabel` and `volumeLCD` will be updated with the current value of `volumeDial`. All this happens at the same time without the application clogging up, all thanks to the efficient design of signals and slots.

Compile and run the project. A typical output of the program is as follows:

In the preceding screenshot, when the `QDial` widget (that is the round-looking object) was moved to **32**, both `volumeLabel` and `volumeLCD` were updated. As you move the dial, `volumeLabel` and `volumeLCD` will receive the updates by way of signals and will update themselves accordingly.

Single slot, multiple signals

In the next example, we shall connect two signals from different widgets to a single slot. Let's modify our earlier program as follows:

```
#include <QApplication>
#include <QVBoxLayout>
#include <QLabel>
#include <QDial>
#include <QSlider>
#include <QLCDNumber>
int main(int argc, char *argv[])
{
    QApplication app(argc, argv);
    QWidget *window = new QWidget;
    QVBoxLayout *layout = new QVBoxLayout;
    QDial *volumeDial= new QDial;
    QSlider *lengthSlider = new QSlider(Qt::Horizontal);
    QLCDNumber *volumeLCD = new QLCDNumber;
    volumeLCD->setPalette(Qt::red);
    lengthSlider->setTickPosition(QSlider::TicksAbove);
    lengthSlider->setTickInterval(10);
    lengthSlider->setSingleStep(1);
```

```
        lengthSlider->setMinimum(0);
        lengthSlider->setMaximum(100);
        volumeDial->setNotchesVisible(true);
        volumeDial->setMinimum(0);
        volumeDial->setMaximum(100);
        layout->addWidget(volumeDial);
        layout->addWidget(lengthSlider);
        layout->addWidget(volumeLCD);
        QObject::connect(volumeDial, SIGNAL(valueChanged(int)), volumeLCD ,
        SLOT(display(int)));
        QObject::connect(lengthSlider, SIGNAL(valueChanged(int)), volumeLCD
        , SLOT(display(int)));
        window->setLayout(layout);
        window->show();
        return app.exec();
    }
```

In the `include` statements, we add the line, `#include <QSlider>`, to add
the `QSlider` class, which is a widget that can be set to a value within a given range:

```
    QApplication app(argc, argv);
    QWidget *window = new QWidget;
    QVBoxLayout *layout = new QVBoxLayout;
    QDial *volumeDial= new QDial;
    QSlider *lengthSlider = new QSlider(Qt::Horizontal);
    QLCDNumber *volumeLCD = new QLCDNumber;
    volumeLCD->setPalette(Qt::red);
```

The `QSlider` widget is instantiated and passed `Qt::Horizontal`, which is a constant that
changes the orientation of the widgets such that it is presented horizontally. Everything else
is the same as we saw in previous examples. The window and layout are instantiated,
together with the `QDial` and `QSlider` objects:

```
    lengthSlider->setTickPosition(QSlider::TicksAbove);
    lengthSlider->setTickInterval(10);
    lengthSlider->setSingleStep(1);
    lengthSlider->setMinimum(0);
```

The first widget that shall emit a signal in this example is the `volumeDial` object. But now,
the `QSlider` instance also emits a signal that allows us to get the state of the `QSlider`
whenever it has changed.

To show the graduations on `QSlider`, we invoke the `setTickPosition()` method and
pass the constant, `QSlider::TicksAbove`. This will show the graduations on top of the
slider, very similar to how the graduations on a straight edge appear.

The setMinimum() and setMaximum() variables are used to set the range of values for our QSlider instance. The range here is between 0 and 100.

The setTickInterval(10) method on the lengthSlider object is used to set the interval between the ticks.

The QVBoxLayout object, layout, adds the lengthSlider widget object to the list of widgets it will house with the line, layout->addWidget(lengthSlider);:

```
QObject::connect(volumeDial, SIGNAL(valueChanged(int)), volumeLCD ,
SLOT(display(int)));
QObject::connect(lengthSlider, SIGNAL(valueChanged(int)), volumeLCD ,
SLOT(display(int)));
```

There are two calls to the static method, connect(). The first call will establish a connection between the valueChanged(int) signal of volumeDial with the display(int) slot of volumeLCD. As a result, whenever the QDial object changes, the value will be passed to the display(int) slot for display.

From a different object, we shall connect the valueChanged(int) signal of lengthSlider to the same slot, display(), of the volumeLCD object.

The remainder of the program is the same as usual.

Compile and run the program from the command line as we have done for the previous examples.

The first time the application is run, the output should be similar to the following:

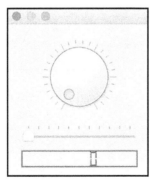

Both QDial and QSlider are at zero. Now, we will move the QDial to **48**. See how the QLCDNumber is updated accordingly:

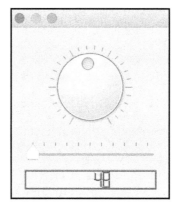

With the way we have set up our signals and slots, it will also be possible for QSlider to also update the same widget, volumeLCD. When we move QSlider, we will see that volumeLCD is updated immediately by its value:

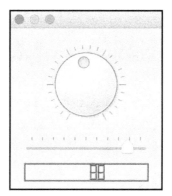

As can be seen, QSlider has been moved to the tail end of its range and the value has been passed onto volumeLCD.

Summary

In this chapter, we took a look at the core concept of signals and slots in Qt. After creating our first application, we looked at the various ways in which signals and slots can be connected.

We saw how to connect one signal from a widget to multiple slots. This is a typical way to set up signals and slots, especially when a change in the state of a widget has to be communicated to many other widgets.

To show how flexible signals and slots could be configured, we also looked at an example where multiple signals were connected to one slot of a widget. This type of arrangement is useful when different widgets can be used to achieve the same effect on a widget.

In Chapter 4, *Implementing Windows and Dialog*, we shall change our style of writing applications and study how to make full-blown window applications.

4
Implementing Windows and Dialog

In the previous chapter, we learned how to animate our application by using signals and slots to trigger and respond to actions that occur within our application. So far, we have been concentrating on examples that are contained in only one file and do not expressly describe a full working application. To do so, we will need to change the style in which our applications are written, and also adopt a number of new conventions.

In this chapter, we shall work with Windows in Qt, so that by the end of the chapter, you should be able to do the following:

- Understand how to subclass and create a custom window application
- Add a menu bar to a window
- Add a toolbar to a window
- Use the various dialog (boxes) to communicate information to the user

Creating a custom window

To create a window(ed) application, we usually call the `show()` method on an instance of `QWidget` and that makes that widget, to be contained in a window of its own, along with its child widgets displayed in it.

A recap of such a simple application is as follows:

```
#include <QApplication>
#include <QMainWindow>
#include <QLabel>
int main(int argc, char *argv[])
{
    QApplication a(argc, argv);
    QMainWindow mainWindow;
```

```
        mainWindow.show();
        return a.exec();
    }
```

`mainWindow` here is an instance of `QMainWindow`, which is derived from `QWidget`. As such, by calling the `show()` method, a window will appear. If you were to replace `QMainWindow` with `QLabel`, this will still work.

But this style of writing applications is not the best. Instead, from this point onward, we shall define our own custom widget, in which we shall define child widgets and make connections between signals and sockets.

Now, let's rewrite the preceding application by sub-classing `QMainWindow`. We have chosen to subclass `QMainWindow` because we need to illustrate the menu and toolbars.

We start off by creating a new folder and defining a header file. The name of our header file here is `mainwindow.h`, but feel free to name it how you want and remember to add the `.h` suffix. This file should basically contain the following:

```
#ifndef MAINWINDOW_H
#define MAINWINDOW_H
#include <QMainWindow>
#include <QLabel>
class MainWindow : public QMainWindow
{
    Q_OBJECT
    public:
        MainWindow();
};
#endif
```

We include the Qt classes `QMainWindow`, and `QLabel` in our header file. Then, we subclass `QMainWindow` and call it `MainWindow`. The constructor of this new class is declared with the following:

```
public:
    MainWindow();
```

The entire class definition is wrapped within an `#ifndef` ... `#endif` directive, which tells the preprocessor to ignore its content if it is accidentally included multiple times in a file.

It is possible to use the non-standard, but widely used, preprocessor directive, #pragma once.

Take notice of the Q_OBJECT macro. This is what makes the signals and slots mechanism possible. Remember that the C++ language does not know about the keywords used to set up signals and slots. By including this macro, it becomes part of the C++ syntax.

What we have defined so far is just the header file. The body of the main program has to live in some other .cpp file. For easy identification, we call it mainwindow.cpp. Create this file within the same folder and add the following lines of code:

```
#include "mainwindow.h"
MainWindow::MainWindow()
{
    setWindowTitle("Main Window");
    resize(400, 700);
    QLabel *mainLabel = new QLabel("Main Widget");
    setCentralWidget(mainLabel);
    mainLabel->setAlignment(Qt::AlignCenter);
}
```

We include the header file that we defined earlier with the first line of code. The default constructor of our sub-classed widget, MainWindow, is defined.

Notice how we call the method that sets the title of the window. setWindowTitle() is invoked and can be accessed from within the constructor since it is an inherited method from QWindow. There is no need to use the this keyword. The size of the window is specified by calling the resize() method and passing two integer values to be used as the dimensions of the window.

An instance of a QLabel is created, mainLabel. The text within the label is aligned to the center by calling mainLabel->setAlignment(Qt::AlignCenter).

A call to setCentralWidget() is important as it situates any class that inherits from QWidget to occupy the interior of the window. Here, mainLabel is being passed to setCentralWidget, and that will make it the only widget to be displayed within the window.

Consider the structure of QMainWindow in the following diagram:

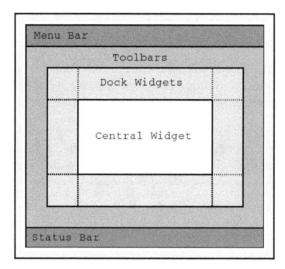

At the very top of every window is the **Menu Bar**. Elements such as the file, edit, and help menus go there. Below that, are the **Toolbars**. Contained within the **Toolbars** are the **Dock Widgets**, which are collapsible panels. Now, the main controls within the window must be put in the **Central Widget** location. Since a UI is made up of several widgets, it will be good to compose a widget that will contain child widgets. This parent widget is what you will stick into the **Central Widget** area. To do this, we call setCentralWidget() and pass in the parent widget. At the bottom of the window, is the **Status Bar**.

To run the application, we need to create an instance of our custom window class. Create a file called main.cpp within the same folder where the header and .cpp files are located. Add the following lines of code to main.cpp:

```
#include <QApplication>
#include "mainwindow.h"
int main(int argc, char *argv[])
{
    QApplication app(argc, argv);
    MainWindow mainwindow;
    mainwindow.show();
    return app.exec();
}
```

We include the header file mainwindow.h, which contains the declaration of our custom class, MainWindow. Without this, the compiler wouldn't know where to find the definition of the MainWindow class.

An instance of `MainWindow` is created and the `show()` method is called on it. We still have to call the `show()` method on `mainwindow`. `MainWindow`, which is a subclass of `QMainWindow`, and behaves just like any widget out there. Furthermore, as we already know, to cause a widget to appear, you have to call the `show()` method on it.

To run the program, move into the folder via the command line and issue the following commands:

```
% qmake -project
```

Add `QT += widgets` to the `.pro` file that is generated. Now continue with the next set of commands:

```
% qmake
% make
```

Examine the `.pro` file for a second. At the very bottom of the file, we have the following lines:

```
HEADERS += mainwindow.h
SOURCES += main.cpp mainwindow.cpp
```

The headers are automatically collected and added to `HEADERS`. Similarly, the `.cpp` files are collected and added to `SOURCES`. Always remember to check this file when there are compilation errors to ensure that all required files have been added.

To run the program, issue the following command:

```
% ./classSimpleWindow
```

For those who work on the macOS, the correct command you will need to issue in order to run the executable is as follows:

```
% ./classSimpleWindow.app/Contents/MacOS/classSimpleWindow
```

The running application should appear, as follows:

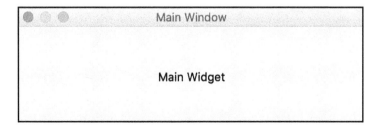

Menu bar

Most applications hold a set of clickable(s) that reveal a list of another set of actions that expose more functionality to the user. The most popular among these are the File, Edit, and Help menus.

In Qt, menu bars occupy the very top of the window. We shall create a short program to make use of the menu bar.

Three files must be created in a newly created folder. These are as follows:

- `main.cpp`
- `mainwindow.h`
- `mainwindow.cpp`

The `main.cpp` file will remain as before in terms of content. Therefore, copy the `main.cpp` file from the previous section. Let's examine the `mainwindow.h` file:

```
#ifndef MAINWINDOW_H
#define MAINWINDOW_H
#include <QMainWindow>
#include <QApplication>
#include <QAction>
#include <QtGui>
#include <QAction>
#include <QMenuBar>
#include <QMenu>
#include <Qt>
class MainWindow : public QMainWindow
{
    Q_OBJECT
    public:
        MainWindow();
    private slots:
    private:
        // Menus
        QMenu *fileMenu;
        QMenu *helpMenu;
        // Actions
        QAction *quitAction;
        QAction *aboutAction;
        QAction *saveAction;
        QAction *cancelAction;
        QAction *openAction;
        QAction *newAction;
        QAction *aboutQtAction;
```

```
};
#endif
```

Once more, the header file is enclosed in an `ifndef` directive to prevent errors that may occur as a result of multiple inclusions of this file.

To create a menu within the window, you need instances of `QMenu`. Each menu, such as the **File** menu, will have sub-menus or items that make up the menu. The **File** menu usually has the **Open**, **New**, and **Close** sub-menus.

A typical image of a **Menu** bar is as follows, with the **File**, **Edit**, and **Help** menus. The File menu items under the **File** menu are **New...**, **Open...**, **Save**, **Save As...**, and **Quit**:

Our application will have only two menus, namely, `fileMenu` and `helpMenu`. The other instances of `QAction` are the individual menu items: `quitAction`, `saveAction`, `cancelAction`, and `newAction`.

Both the menu and sub-menu items are defined as members of the class in the header file. Furthermore, this kind of declaration will allow users to modify their behavior and also to easily access them when connecting them to sockets.

Now, let's switch to the `mainwindow.cpp`. Copy the following code into `mainwindow.cpp`:

```cpp
#include "mainwindow.h"
MainWindow::MainWindow()
{
    setWindowTitle("SRM System");
    setFixedSize(500, 500);
    QPixmap newIcon("new.png");
    QPixmap openIcon("open.png");
    QPixmap closeIcon("close.png");
    // Setup File Menu
    fileMenu = menuBar()->addMenu("&File");
    quitAction = new QAction(closeIcon, "Quit", this);
```

```
    quitAction->setShortcuts(QKeySequence::Quit);
    newAction = new QAction(newIcon, "&New", this);
    newAction->setShortcut(QKeySequence(Qt::CTRL + Qt::Key_C));
    openAction = new QAction(openIcon, "&New", this);
    openAction->setShortcut(QKeySequence(Qt::CTRL + Qt::Key_O));
    fileMenu->addAction(newAction);
    fileMenu->addAction(openAction);
    fileMenu->addSeparator();
    fileMenu->addAction(quitAction);
    helpMenu = menuBar()->addMenu("Help");
    aboutAction = new QAction("About", this);
    aboutAction->setShortcut(QKeySequence(Qt::CTRL + Qt::Key_H));
    helpMenu->addAction(aboutAction);
    // Setup Signals and Slots
    connect(quitAction, &QAction::triggered, this, &QApplication::quit);
}
```

The header file, `mainwindow.h`, is included at the beginning of the file to make available the class declaration and Qt classes that will be used in the program.

In the default constructor of our custom class, `MainWindow`, we start by setting the name of our window by calling `setWindowTitle()` and giving it an appropriate name. The size of our window is then established by calling `setFixedSize()`. This is demonstrated in the following code block:

```
QPixmap newIcon("new.png");
QPixmap openIcon("open.png");
QPixmap closeIcon("close.png");
```

Menu items can be displayed with images beside them. To associate an image or icon with a menu item, `QAction`, you need to first capture that image within an instance of `QPixmap`. Three such images are captured in the `newIcon`, `openIcon`, and `closeIcon` variables. These will be used further down the code.

Let's set up the `fileMenu` as follows:

```
fileMenu = menuBar()->addMenu("&File");
quitAction = new QAction(closeIcon, "Quit", this);
quitAction->setShortcuts(QKeySequence::Quit);
```

To add a menu to the window, a call to `menuBar()` is made. This returns an instance of `QMenu`, and we call `addMenu` on that object specifying the name of the menu we want to add. Here, we call our first menu, **File**. The "`&`" sign in front of the **F** in **File** will make it possible to press *Alt + F* on the keyboard.

`quitAction` is passed an instance of `QAction()`. `closeIcon` is the image we want to associate with this sub-menu. `"Quit"` is the display name and the `this` keyword makes the `quitAction` a child widget of `MainWindow`.

A shortcut to a sub-menu is associated with `quitAction` by calling `setShortcuts()`. By using `QKeySequence::Quit`, we mask the need to cater for platform-specific key sequences that are used.

`newAction` and `openAction` follow the same logic in their creation.

Now that we have our menu in `fileMenu` and the menu items in `quitAction`, `newAction`, and `openActions`, we need to link them together:

```
fileMenu->addAction(newAction);
fileMenu->addAction(openAction);
fileMenu->addSeparator();
fileMenu->addAction(quitAction);
```

To add a sub-menu item, we call the `addAction()` method on the `QMenu` instance, `fileMenu`, and pass the required `QAction` instance. The `addSeparator()` is used to insert a visual marker in our list of menu items. It also returns an instance of `QAction`, but we are not interested in that object at this moment.

A second menu is added to the application along with its only sub-menu item:

```
helpMenu = menuBar()->addMenu("Help");
aboutAction = new QAction("About", this);
aboutAction->setShortcut(QKeySequence(Qt::CTRL + Qt::Key_H));
helpMenu->addAction(aboutAction);
```

`QAction` encapsulates a general idea of an action that can be inserted into widgets. Here, we used `QAction` to insert actions into our menus.

These `QAction` instances emit the `triggered` signal, which can be connected to a socket to cause the application to change, as follows:

```
connect(quitAction, &QAction::triggered, this, &QApplication::quit);
```

When connecting a signal to a slot within a class definition, simply call the `connect()` method and pass in the parameters as you would do normally. The first parameter is the object that is going to emit the signal we are interested in. `&QAction::triggered` is one way of specifying the triggered signal. This is the same as writing `SIGNAL(triggered())`. The `this` keyword refers to the `MainWindow` object that will be created in the future. The quit slot is specified by `&QApplication::quit`.

The signal and slot connected will create a situation where, when the **File** menu is opened and the **Close** button is clicked, the application will close.

The last file needed to run this example is the main.cpp file. The previous main.cpp file created should be copied over to this project.

Compile and run the project. A typical output should be as follows:

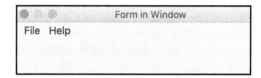

On a Mac, press the key combination *Command + Q* and that will close the application. On Linux and Windows, *Alt + F4* should do the same. This is made possible by the following line of code:

```
quitAction->setShortcuts(QKeySequence::Quit);
```

This line of code blurs out the difference by relying on Qt's QKeySequence::Quit, depending on the OS in use.

Click on the **File** menu and select **New**:

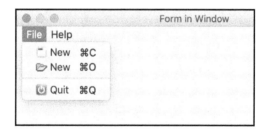

Nothing happens. That is because we did not define what should happen when the user clicks on that action. The last menu item, **Quit**, on the other hand, closes the application as defined by the socket and slot we declared.

Also, take note of how each menu item has an appropriate icon or image in front of it.

Visit the Packt website to obtain the images for this book.

Toolbar

Beneath the menu bar is a panel that is usually referred to as toolbar. It contains a set of controls that could be widgets or instances of QAction, just as we saw in their use in creating the menu bar. This also means that you may choose to replace the QAction with a widget, such as a regular QPushButton or QComboBox.

Toolbars may be fixed to the top of the window (beneath the menu bar) and can be pinned there or made to float around the dock widget.

Once again, we will need to create a new project or modify the one from the previous section of this chapter. The files that we will be creating are main.cpp, mainwindow.h, and mainwindow.cpp.

The main.cpp file remains the same, as follows. We only instantiate our custom class and call show() on it:

```cpp
#include <QApplication>
#include "mainwindow.h"
int main(int argc, char *argv[])
{
    QApplication app(argc, argv);
    QCoreApplication::setAttribute(Qt::AA_DontUseNativeMenuBar); //
    MainWindow mainwindow;
    mainwindow.show();
    return app.exec();
}
```

The mainwindow.h file will essentially contain the QAction members that will hold the actions in our toolbar:

```cpp
#ifndef MAINWINDOW_H
#define MAINWINDOW_H
#include <QMainWindow>
#include <QApplication>
#include <QAction>
#include <QPushButton>
#include <QAction>
#include <QMenuBar>
#include <QMenu>
#include <QtGui>
#include <Qt>
#include <QToolBar>
#include <QTableView>
class MainWindow : public QMainWindow
{
```

```
      Q_OBJECT
      public:
          MainWindow();
      private slots:
      private:
          // Menus
          QMenu *fileMenu;
          QMenu *helpMenu;
          // Actions
          QAction *quitAction;
          QAction *aboutAction;
          QAction *saveAction;
          QAction *cancelAction;
          QAction *openAction;
          QAction *newAction;
          QAction *aboutQtAction;
          QToolBar *toolbar;
          QAction *newToolBarAction;
          QAction *openToolBarAction;
          QAction *closeToolBarAction;
      };
      #endif
```

This header file appears the same as before. The only difference is the QToolbar instance, *toolbar, and the QAction objects that will be shown within the toolbar. These are newToolBarAction, openToolBarAction, and closeToolBarAction. The QAction instances that are used in a menu are the same as the ones used for toolbars.

Note that there are no slots being declared.

The mainwindow.cpp file will contain the following:

```
#include "mainwindow.h"
MainWindow::MainWindow()
{
    setWindowTitle("Form in Window");
    setFixedSize(500, 500);
    QPixmap newIcon("new.png");
    QPixmap openIcon("open.png");
    QPixmap closeIcon("close.png");
    // Setup File Menu
    fileMenu = menuBar()->addMenu("&File");
    quitAction = new QAction(closeIcon, "Quit", this);
    quitAction->setShortcuts(QKeySequence::Quit);
    newAction = new QAction(newIcon, "&New", this);
    newAction->setShortcut(QKeySequence(Qt::CTRL + Qt::Key_C));
    openAction = new QAction(openIcon, "&New", this);
```

```
    openAction->setShortcut(QKeySequence(Qt::CTRL + Qt::Key_O));
    fileMenu->addAction(newAction);
    fileMenu->addAction(openAction);
    fileMenu->addSeparator();
    fileMenu->addAction(quitAction);
    helpMenu = menuBar()->addMenu("Help");
    aboutAction = new QAction("About", this);
    aboutAction->setShortcut(QKeySequence(Qt::CTRL + Qt::Key_H));
    helpMenu->addAction(aboutAction);
    // Setup Tool bar menu
    toolbar = addToolBar("main toolbar");
    // toolbar->setMovable( false );
    newToolBarAction = toolbar->addAction(QIcon(newIcon), "New File");
    openToolBarAction = toolbar->addAction(QIcon(openIcon), "Open File");
    toolbar->addSeparator();
    closeToolBarAction = toolbar->addAction(QIcon(closeIcon), "Quit
Application");
    // Setup Signals and Slots
    connect(quitAction, &QAction::triggered, this, &QApplication::quit);
    connect(closeToolBarAction, &QAction::triggered, this,
&QApplication::quit);
}
```

The same set of icons used for the menu bar will be used for the toolbars too.

To obtain an instance of the Windows toolbar for further manipulation, call the
addTooBar() method, which will return an instance of a QToolBar. The method accepts
any text that is used as the title of the window. It also adds the toolbar to the window.

The toolbar at this point can be moved around within the window. To fix it to the top of the
window, call the toolbar->setMovable(false); function on the instance of the
QToolBar, toolbar:

```
    newToolBarAction = toolbar->addAction(QIcon(newIcon), "New File");
    openToolBarAction = toolbar->addAction(QIcon(openIcon), "Open File");
    toolbar->addSeparator();
    closeToolBarAction = toolbar->addAction(QIcon(closeIcon), "Quit
    Application");
```

Two QAction objects are created and passed to the newToolBarAction and
openToolBarAction objects. We pass the QIcon object that becomes the image on the
QAction and a name or text to be displayed as a tooltip. A separator is added to the toolbar
by calling the addSeparator() method. The last control, closeToolBarAction, contains
an image to be displayed on the toolbar.

To link the trigger signal of `closeToolBarAction` to the quit slot of the window, we do the following:

```
connect(closeToolBarAction, &QAction::triggered, this,
&QApplication::quit);
```

To compile this project as a recap, run the following commands:

```
% qmake -project
```

Add `QT += widgets` to the `.pro` file that is generated and make sure all three files are listed in the bottom of the file:

Proceed to issue the following commands in order to build the project:

```
% qmake
% make
% ./name_of_executable
```

If everything went well, you will see the following:

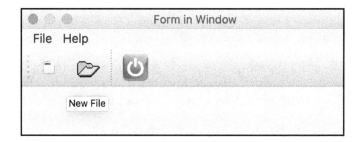

The preceding screenshot shows the toolbar beneath the **File** and **Help** menus. Three icons show three `QAction` objects that represent the **New**, **Open**, and **Close** actions. Only the last button (to close the application) action works. That is because we only defined a single signal-slot connection for the `closeToolBarAction` and `QAction` objects.

By hovering the mouse over the toolbar menu items, some text appears. This message is called a tooltip. As can be seen in the preceding diagram, the Open File message is derived from the last parameter of the following line:

```
openToolBarAction = toolbar->addAction(QIcon(openIcon), "Open File");
```

As noted earlier, a toolbar can be moved around within a window as follows:

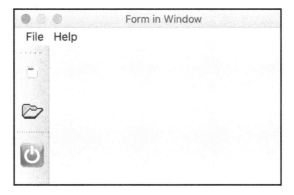

As you can see, by clicking on the three vertical dots on the left-hand side of the toolbar and moving it, you can detach the toolbar from the top to either the left, right, or bottom. To display this kind of functionality, issue the following command:

```
toolbar->setMovable(false);
```

This will fix the toolbar to the top so that it can't be moved around.

Adding other widgets

So far, we have only added a menu bar and a toolbar to our window. To add other widgets that might make our application useful, we have to add more members to our header file. In this section, we shall create a simple application that appends personal details to a displayable list.

There will be a form where the details of a number of contacts will be received. This detail will then be added to a list on the window. As more contacts are added, the list will grow. We shall base these on the previous section's code and continue to build on it.

As usual, you create a new folder with the three files, namely, main.cpp, mainwindow.cpp, and mainwindow.h. The main.cpp file will remain as before from the previous sections.

The mainwindow.h file should contain the following lines of code:

```
#ifndef MAINWINDOW_H
#define MAINWINDOW_H
#include <QMainWindow>
#include <QApplication>
```

```
#include <QLabel>
#include <QLineEdit>
#include <QDate>
#include <QDateEdit>
#include <QVBoxLayout>
#include <QHBoxLayout>
#include <QGridLayout>
#include <QPushButton>
#include <QMessageBox>
#include <QAction>
#include <QMenuBar>
#include <QMenu>
#include <QtGui>
#include <Qt>
#include <QToolBar>
#include <QTableView>
#include <QHeaderView>
```

The file imports the classes that will be used in declaring the members within our custom class. The whole file is wrapped with the `#ifndef` directive so that the header file can be included multiple times without yielding errors.

Add the following lines of code to the same header file, `mainwindow.h`:

```
class MainWindow : public QMainWindow
{
    Q_OBJECT
public:
    MainWindow();
private slots:
    void saveButtonClicked();
```

We then declare our default constructor for our class.

There is only one slot in our application that will be used to move the content of a number of widgets into a list.

Continue the code listing by adding the following lines of code that will add the members of the class and define the prototype of some `helper` methods:

```
private:
    // Widgets
    QWidget *mainWidget;
    QVBoxLayout *centralWidgetLayout;
    QGridLayout *formLayout;
    QHBoxLayout *buttonsLayout;
    QLabel *nameLabel;
    QLabel *dateOfBirthLabel;
```

```
    QLabel *phoneNumberLabel;
    QPushButton *savePushButton;
    QPushButton *newPushButton;
    QLineEdit *nameLineEdit;
    QDateEdit *dateOfBirthEdit;
    QLineEdit *phoneNumberLineEdit;
    QTableView *appTable;
    QStandardItemModel *model;
    // Menus
    QMenu *fileMenu;
    QMenu *helpMenu;
    // Actions
    QAction *quitAction;
    QAction *aboutAction;
    QAction *saveAction;
    QAction *cancelAction;
    QAction *openAction;
    QAction *newAction;
    QAction *aboutQtAction;
    QAction *newToolBarAction;
    QAction *openToolBarAction;
    QAction *closeToolBarAction;
    QAction *clearToolBarAction;
    // Toolbar
    QToolBar *toolbar;
    // Icons
    QPixmap newIcon;
    QPixmap openIcon;
    QPixmap closeIcon;
    QPixmap clearIcon;
    // init methods
    void clearFields();
    void createIcons();
    void createMenuBar();
    void createToolBar();
    void setupSignalsAndSlot();
    void setupCoreWidgets();
};
#endif
```

The members include layout and other widget classes, classes for our menu, toolbars, and their associated QAction objects.

As you can see, the code is borrowed from the previous section with the exception of the widgets being added.

The private methods, `createIcons()`, `createMenuBar()`, `createToolBar()`, `setupSignalsAndSlot()`, and `setupCoreWidgets()`, will be used to refactor the code that should live in our default constructor. The `clearFields()` method will be used to clear the data from a number of widgets.

In the `mainwindow.cpp` file, we shall define our class with the following lines of code:

```cpp
#include "mainwindow.h"
#include "mainwindow.h"
MainWindow::MainWindow()
{
    setWindowTitle("Form in Window");
    setFixedSize(500, 500);
    createIcons();
    setupCoreWidgets();
    createMenuBar();
    createToolBar();
    centralWidgetLayout->addLayout(formLayout);
    centralWidgetLayout->addWidget(appTable);
    centralWidgetLayout->addLayout(buttonsLayout);
    mainWidget->setLayout(centralWidgetLayout);
    setCentralWidget(mainWidget);
    setupSignalsAndSlots();
}
```

The default constructor has been refactored a great deal here. The building blocks of code have been moved away into functions to help make the code readable.

Now, we only set the window title and size of the application window. Next, we call the method that will create the icons that will be used by the various widgets. Another function call is made to set up the core widgets by calling the `setupCoreWidgets()` method. The menu and toolbars are created by calling the `createMenuBar()` and `createToolBar()` methods.

The layout object, `centralWidgetLayout`, is the main layout of our application. We add the `formLayout` object first, followed by the `appTable` object. As you can see, it is possible to insert a layout into another layout. Lastly, we insert the `buttonsLayout` object, which contains our buttons.

The `mainWidget` object's layout is set to `centralWidgetLayout`. This `mainWidget` object is then set as the main widget that should occupy the center of the window, as was demonstrated in the first diagram of this chapter.

All signals and slots will be set up in the `setupSignalsAndSlot()` method.

Add the following lines of code to the `mainwindow.cpp` file that defines the `createIcons()` method:

```
void MainWindow::createIcons() {
    newIcon = QPixmap("new.png");
    openIcon = QPixmap("open.png");
    closeIcon = QPixmap("close.png");
    clearIcon = QPixmap("clear.png");
}
```

The `createIcons()` method will pass instances of `QPixmap` to the members that were declared in `mainwindow.h`.

The definition of `setupCoreWidgets()` is as follows, in `mainwindow.cpp`:

```
void MainWindow::setupCoreWidgets() {
    mainWidget = new QWidget();
    centralWidgetLayout = new QVBoxLayout();
    formLayout = new QGridLayout();
    buttonsLayout = new QHBoxLayout();
    nameLabel = new QLabel("Name:");
    dateOfBirthLabel= new QLabel("Date Of Birth:");
    phoneNumberLabel = new QLabel("Phone Number");
    savePushButton = new QPushButton("Save");
    newPushButton = new QPushButton("Clear All");
    nameLineEdit = new QLineEdit();
    dateOfBirthEdit = new QDateEdit(QDate::currentDate());
    phoneNumberLineEdit = new QLineEdit();
    // TableView
    appTable = new QTableView();
    model = new QStandardItemModel(1, 3, this);
    appTable->setContextMenuPolicy(Qt::CustomContextMenu);
appTable->horizontalHeader()->setSectionResizeMode(QHeaderView::Stretch);
/** Note **/
    model->setHorizontalHeaderItem(0, new QStandardItem(QString("Name")));
    model->setHorizontalHeaderItem(1, new QStandardItem(QString("Date of
Birth")));
    model->setHorizontalHeaderItem(2, new QStandardItem(QString("Phone
Number")));    appTable->setModel(model)

    QStandardItem *firstItem = new QStandardItem(QString("G. Shone"));
    QDate dateOfBirth(1980, 1, 1);
    QStandardItem *secondItem = new QStandardItem(dateOfBirth.toString());
    QStandardItem *thirdItem = new QStandardItem(QString("05443394858"));
    model->setItem(0,0,firstItem);
    model->setItem(0,1,secondItem);
    model->setItem(0,2,thirdItem);
    formLayout->addWidget(nameLabel, 0, 0);
```

```
        formLayout->addWidget(nameLineEdit, 0, 1);
        formLayout->addWidget(dateOfBirthLabel, 1, 0);
        formLayout->addWidget(dateOfBirthEdit, 1, 1);
        formLayout->addWidget(phoneNumberLabel, 2, 0);
        formLayout->addWidget(phoneNumberLineEdit, 2, 1);
        buttonsLayout->addStretch();
        buttonsLayout->addWidget(savePushButton);
        buttonsLayout->addWidget(newPushButton);
    }
```

Here, we are just instantiating objects to be used within the application. There is nothing out of the ordinary here. `nameLineEdit` and `phoneNumberLineEdit` will be used to collect the name and phone number of contacts about to be saved. `dateOfBirthEdit` is a special kind of textbox that allows you to specify a date. `savePushButton` and `newPushButton` are buttons that will be used to trigger the saving of the contact and the clearing of the list.

The labels and line edit controls will be used in the `formLayout` object, which is a `QGridLayout` instance. `QGridLayout` allows widgets to be specified using columns and rows.

To save a contact, this means we will save it to a widget that can display a list of items. Qt has a number of such widgets. These include `QListView`, `QTableView`, and `QTreeView`.

When the `QListView` is used in displaying information, it will typically appear as in the following screenshot:

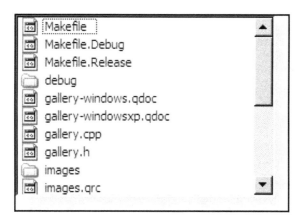

QTableView will use columns and rows to display data or information in cells as follows:

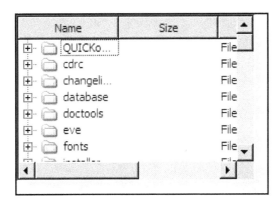

To show hierarchical information, QTreeView is also used, as in the following screenshot:

An instance of QTableView is passed to appTable. We need a model for our QTableView instance. The model will hold the data that will be displayed in our table. When data is added or removed from the model, its corresponding view will be updated to show the change that has occurred, automatically. The model here is an instance of QStandardItemModel. The line QStandardItemModel(1, 3, this) will create an instance with one row and three columns. The this keyword is used to make the model a child of the MainWindow object:

```
appTable->setContextMenuPolicy(Qt::CustomContextMenu);
```

This line is used to help us define a custom action that should happen when we raise a context menu on the table:

```
appTable->horizontalHeader()->setSectionResizeMode(
QHeaderView::Stretch); /** Note **/
```

The preceding line is important and enables the headers of our table to stretch out fully. This is the result when we omit that line (as shown in an area bounded by the red box):

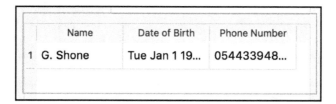

Ideally, we want our table to have the following header, so that it looks like this:

	Name	Date of Birth	Phone Number
1	G. Shone	Tue Jan 1 1980	05443394858

To set the header for the table, we can do so with the following lines of code:

```
model->setHorizontalHeaderItem(0, new QStandardItem(QString("Name")));
```

The table for displaying the contacts needs headers. The setHorizontalHeaderItem() method on the model object uses the first parameter to indicate the position where the new QStandardItem(QString()) should be inserted. Because our table uses three columns, the line is repeated three times for the headers, **Name**, **Date of Birth**, and **Phone Number**:

```
appTable->setModel(model);
QStandardItem *firstItem = new QStandardItem(QString("G. Shone"));
QDate dateOfBirth(1980, 1, 1);
QStandardItem *secondItem = new QStandardItem(dateOfBirth.toString());
QStandardItem *thirdItem = new QStandardItem(QString("05443394858"));
model->setItem(0,0,firstItem);
model->setItem(0,1,secondItem);
model->setItem(0,2,thirdItem);
```

We make model the model of our QTableView by calling setModel() on appTable and passing model as a parameter.

To populate our model, which updates its view, QTableView, we shall create instances of QStandardItem. Each cell in our table has to be encapsulated in this class. dateOfBirth is of the QDate type, so we call toString() on it and pass it to new QStandardItem(). firstItem is inserted into our model by specifying the row and column as in the line model->setItem(0, 0, firstItem);.

This is done for the second and third `QStandardItem` objects.

Now, let's populate our `formLayout` object. This is of the `QGridLayout` type. To insert widgets into our layout, use the following lines of code:

```
formLayout->addWidget(nameLabel, 0, 0);
formLayout->addWidget(nameLineEdit, 0, 1);
formLayout->addWidget(dateOfBirthLabel, 1, 0);
formLayout->addWidget(dateOfBirthEdit, 1, 1);
formLayout->addWidget(phoneNumberLabel, 2, 0);
formLayout->addWidget(phoneNumberLineEdit, 2, 1);
```

We add widgets to the layout by calling `addWidget()`, supplying the widget, and the row and column it is supposed to fill. `0, 0` will fill the first cell, `0, 1` will fill the second cell on the first row, and `1, 0` will fill the first cell on the second row.

The following code adds buttons to the `QHBoxLayout` instance of `buttonsLayout`:

```
buttonsLayout->addStretch();
buttonsLayout->addWidget(savePushButton);
buttonsLayout->addWidget(newPushButton);
```

To push `savePushButton` and `newPushButton` to the right, we first add a stretch that will expand and fill the empty space by calling `addStretch()` before a call to add the widgets is made by `addWidget()`.

Before we come to the menus in the application, add the following code. To include menus and a toolbar to our application, add the definition of `createMenuBar()` and `createToolBar()` to the `mainwindow.cpp` file:

```cpp
void MainWindow::createMenuBar() {
    // Setup File Menu
    fileMenu = menuBar()->addMenu("&File");
    quitAction = new QAction(closeIcon, "Quit", this);
    quitAction->setShortcuts(QKeySequence::Quit);
    newAction = new QAction(newIcon, "&New", this);
    newAction->setShortcut(QKeySequence(Qt::CTRL + Qt::Key_C));
    openAction = new QAction(openIcon, "&New", this);
    openAction->setShortcut(QKeySequence(Qt::CTRL + Qt::Key_O));
    fileMenu->addAction(newAction);
    fileMenu->addAction(openAction);
    fileMenu->addSeparator();
    fileMenu->addAction(quitAction);
    helpMenu = menuBar()->addMenu("Help");
    aboutAction = new QAction("About", this);
    aboutAction->setShortcut(QKeySequence(Qt::CTRL + Qt::Key_H));
    helpMenu->addAction(aboutAction);
```

```
    }
    void MainWindow::createToolBar() {
        // Setup Tool bar menu
        toolbar = addToolBar("main toolbar");
        // toolbar->setMovable( false );
        newToolBarAction = toolbar->addAction(QIcon(newIcon), "New File");
        openToolBarAction = toolbar->addAction(QIcon(openIcon), "Open File");
        toolbar->addSeparator();
        clearToolBarAction = toolbar->addAction(QIcon(clearIcon), "Clear All");
        closeToolBarAction = toolbar->addAction(QIcon(closeIcon), "Quit
    Application");
    }
```

The preceding code is familiar code that adds a toolbar and menus to our window. The final lines of code define the setupSignalsAndSlots() method:

```
    void MainWindow::setupSignalsAndSlots() {
        // Setup Signals and Slots
        connect(quitAction, &QAction::triggered, this, &QApplication::quit);
        connect(closeToolBarAction, &QAction::triggered, this,
    &QApplication::quit);
        connect(savePushButton, SIGNAL(clicked()), this,
    SLOT(saveButtonClicked()));
    }
```

In the preceding code, we connect the triggered signal of quitAction to the quit slot of QApplication. The triggered signal of closeToolBarAction is connected to the same, to achieve the effect of closing the application.

The clicked() signal of savePushButton is connected to the slot, saveButtonClicked(). Because it is defined within our class, the this keyword is used in the third parameter.

The exact operation that ensures that the information input into the form is saved, is defined by the saveButtonClicked() function that serves a slot.

To define our slot, add the following code to `mainwindow.cpp`:

```
void MainWindow::saveButtonClicked()
{
  QStandardItem *name = new QStandardItem(nameLineEdit->text());
  QStandardItem *dob = new
QStandardItem(dateOfBirthEdit->date().toString());
    QStandardItem *phoneNumber = new
QStandardItem(phoneNumberLineEdit->text());
    model->appendRow({ name, dob, phoneNumber});
    clearFields();
}
```

When `saveButtonClicked()` is invoked, we shall extract the values within the controls, `nameLinedEdit`, `dateOfBirthEdit`, and `phoneNumberLineEdit`. We append them to the model by calling `appendRow()` on the model object. We can access the model object because it is a member point variable in our class definition.

After appending the new contact information into the list, all the fields are cleared and reset with a call to `clearFields()`.

To clear the fields, we call `clearFields()`, which is defined in `mainwindow.cpp` as follows:

```
void MainWindow::clearFields()
{
    nameLineEdit->clear();
    phoneNumberLineEdit->setText("");
    QDate dateOfBirth(1980, 1, 1);
    dateOfBirthEdit->setDate(dateOfBirth);
}
```

The `nameLineEdit` object is reset to an empty string by calling the `clear()` method. This method also doubles as a slot. Another way to set a `QLineEdit` object to an empty string is by setting the text to `""` by calling the `setText("")`:

Because `QDateEdit` accepts dates, we have to create an instance of `date` and pass it to `setDate()` of `dateOfBirthEdit`.

Compile and run the project. You should see the following output:

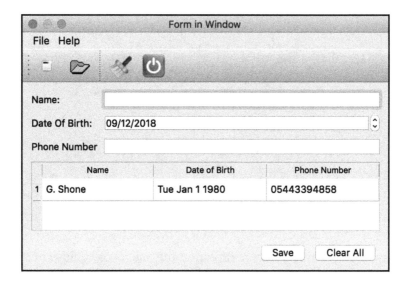

To add a new contact, complete the form and click on the **Save** button:

After clicking on the **Save** button, you should see the following:

Adding dialog boxes

There are times when an application needs to inform the user of an action or to receive input for further processing. Usually, another window, typically small in size, will appear with such information or instructions. In Qt, the QMessageBox provides us with the functionality to raise alerts and receive input using QInputDialog.

There are different messages, as explained in the following table:

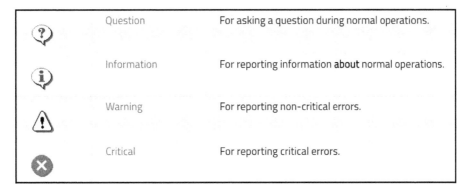

	Question	For asking a question during normal operations.
	Information	For reporting information **about** normal operations.
	Warning	For reporting non-critical errors.
	Critical	For reporting critical errors.

To raise an instance of QMessage to communicate a recently accomplished task to the user, the following code listing can serve as an example:

```
QMessageBox::information(this, tr("RMS System"), tr("Record saved
successfully!"),QMessageBox::Ok|QMessageBox::Default,
QMessageBox::NoButton, QMessageBox::NoButton);
```

The preceding code listing will yield an output such as the following:

This QMessageBox instance is being used to communicate to the user that an operation was successful.

The icon and number of buttons on a QMessageBox instance is configurable.

Let's complete the contact application being written to show how QMessageBox and QInputDialog are used.

Choose to build upon the example in the previous section or create a new folder with the three main files we have been working with so far, that is, main.cpp, mainwindow.cpp, and mainwindow.h.

The mainwindow.h file should contain the following:

```
#ifndef MAINWINDOW_H
#define MAINWINDOW_H
#include <QMainWindow>
#include <QApplication>
#include <QLabel>
#include <QLineEdit>
#include <QDate>
#include <QDateEdit>
#include <QVBoxLayout>
#include <QHBoxLayout>
#include <QGridLayout>
#include <QPushButton>
#include <QMessageBox>
#include <QAction>
```

```cpp
#include <QMenuBar>
#include <QMenu>
#include <QtGui>
#include <Qt>
#include <QToolBar>
#include <QTableView>
#include <QHeaderView>
#include <QInputDialog>
class MainWindow : public QMainWindow
{
    Q_OBJECT
    public:
        MainWindow();
    private slots:
        void saveButtonClicked();
        void aboutDialog();
        void clearAllRecords();
        void deleteSavedRecord();
    private:
        // Widgets
        QWidget *mainWidget;
        QVBoxLayout *centralWidgetLayout;
        QGridLayout *formLayout;
        QHBoxLayout *buttonsLayout;
        QLabel *nameLabel;
        QLabel *dateOfBirthLabel;
        QLabel *phoneNumberLabel;
        QPushButton *savePushButton;
        QPushButton *clearPushButton;
        QLineEdit *nameLineEdit;
        QDateEdit *dateOfBirthEdit;
        QLineEdit *phoneNumberLineEdit;
        QTableView *appTable;
        QStandardItemModel *model;
        // Menus
        QMenu *fileMenu;
        QMenu *helpMenu;
        // Actions
        QAction *quitAction;
        QAction *aboutAction;
        QAction *saveAction;
        QAction *cancelAction;
        QAction *openAction;
        QAction *newAction;
        QAction *aboutQtAction;
        QAction *newToolBarAction;
        QAction *openToolBarAction;
        QAction *closeToolBarAction;
```

```
                        QAction *clearToolBarAction;
                        QAction *deleteOneEntryToolBarAction;
                        // Icons
                        QPixmap newIcon;
                        QPixmap openIcon;
                        QPixmap closeIcon;
                        QPixmap clearIcon;
                        QPixmap deleteIcon;
                        // Toolbar
                        QToolBar *toolbar;
                        void clearFields();
                        void createIcons();
                        void createMenuBar();
                        void createToolBar();
                        void setupSignalsAndSlots();
                        void setupCoreWidgets();
            };
            #endif
```

The only notable change is the increase in the number of slots. The `saveButtonClicked()` slot will be reimplemented to pop up a message telling the user of a successful save action. The `aboutDialog()` slot will be used to show an about message. This is usually a window that conveys information about the program and usually contains copyright, help, and contact information.

The `clearAllRecords()` slot will invoke a question message box that will prompt the user of the destructive action about to be taken. `deleteSavedRecord()` will use `QInputDialog` to accept input from the user as to which row to remove from our list of saved contacts.

`QAction *aboutQtAction` will be used to invoke the slot to display the about page or message. We shall also add a toolbar action, `QAction *deleteOneEntryToolBarAction`, that will be used to invoke a dialog box that will receive input from the user. Observe these three inputs, `QPixmap deleteIcon`, `QPixmap clearIcon`, and `QPixmap deleteIcon`, as we add more actions to the window and, likewise, the `QPushButton*clearPushButton`, which is replacing `newPushButton` in the previous example.

Everything else about the header file remains the same. The two extra classes imported are the `QMessageBox` and `QInputDialog` classes.

In the `mainwindow.cpp` file, we define the default constructor of the `MainWindow` class as follows:

```
#include "mainwindow.h"
MainWindow::MainWindow()
```

```
{
    setWindowTitle("RMS System");
    setFixedSize(500, 500);
    setWindowIcon(QIcon("window_logo.png"));
    createIcons();
    setupCoreWidgets();
    createMenuBar();
    createToolBar();
    centralWidgetLayout->addLayout(formLayout);
    centralWidgetLayout->addWidget(appTable);
    //centralWidgetLayout->addStretch();
    centralWidgetLayout->addLayout(buttonsLayout);
    mainWidget->setLayout(centralWidgetLayout);
    setCentralWidget(mainWidget);
    setupSignalsAndSlots();
}
```

This time, we want to give the whole application an icon that will show up in a taskbar or dock when it is running. To do this, we call the `setWindowIcon()` method and pass in an instance of `QIcon("window_logo.png")`.

 The `window_logo.png` file is included in the project, along with the other image files being used as an attachment on the Packt site for this book.

Everything remains the same as before in the previous example. The methods that are setting up the various parts of the application have been modified slightly.

The `setupSignalsAndSlots()` method is implemented with the following lines of code:

```
void MainWindow::setupSignalsAndSlots() {
    // Setup Signals and Slots
    connect(quitAction, &QAction::triggered, this, &QApplication::quit);
    connect(aboutAction, SIGNAL(triggered()), this, SLOT(aboutDialog()));
    connect(clearToolBarAction, SIGNAL(triggered()), this,
SLOT(clearAllRecords()));
    connect(closeToolBarAction, &QAction::triggered, this,
&QApplication::quit);
    connect(deleteOneEntryToolBarAction, SIGNAL(triggered()), this,
SLOT(deleteSavedRecord()));
    connect(savePushButton, SIGNAL(clicked()), this,
SLOT(saveButtonClicked()));
    connect(clearPushButton, SIGNAL(clicked()), this,
SLOT(clearAllRecords()));
}
```

The `triggered()` signal of `aboutAction` is connected to the `aboutDialog()`. slot. This method raises a dialog box that is used to display a window with some information about the application and a logo of the app (which we have defined by calling `setWindowIcon()`):

```
void MainWindow::aboutDialog()
{
    QMessageBox::about(this, "About RMS System","RMS System 2.0"
    "<p>Copyright &copy; 2005 Inc." "This is a simple application to
    demonstrate the use of windows," "tool bars, menus and dialog boxes");
}
```

The static method, `QMessageBox::about()`, is called with `this` as its first argument. The title of the window is the second argument, and a string that describes the application is given as the third parameter.

At runtime, click on the **Help** menu and then click on **About**. You should see the following output:

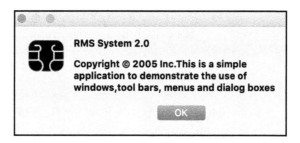

The third signal-slot connection that is established in the `setupSignalsAndSlots()` method is as follows:

```
connect(clearToolBarAction, SIGNAL(triggered()), this,
SLOT(clearAllRecords()));
```

In the `clearAllRecords()` slot, we will first ask the user with the aid of a prompt if they are sure they want all the items in a model to be removed. This can be achieved by the following code:

```
int status = QMessageBox::question( this, tr("Delete Records ?"), tr("You
are about to delete all saved records "
"<p>Are you sure you want to delete all records "),
QMessageBox::No|QMessageBox::Default, QMessageBox::No|QMessageBox::Escape,
QMessageBox::NoButton);
if (status == QMessageBox::Yes)
    return model->clear();
```

`QMessageBox::question` is used to raise a dialog to ask the user a question. It has two main buttons, **Yes** and **No**. `QMessageBox::No|QMessageBox::Default` sets the **No** option as the default selection. `QMessageBox::No|QMessageBox::Escape` makes the escape key have the same effect as clicking on the **No** option.

Whatever option the user chooses will be stored as `int` in the status variable. It will then be compared to the `QMessageBox::Yes` constant. This way of asking the user a **Yes** or **No** question is not informative enough, especially when a destructive operation will ensue when the user clicks **Yes**. We shall use the alternative form as defined in `clearAllRecords()`:

```
void MainWindow::clearAllRecords()
{
    */
    int status = QMessageBox::question( this, tr("Delete all Records ?"),
  tr("This operation will delete all saved records. " "<p>Do you want to
  remove all saved records ? "
  ), tr("Yes, Delete all records"), tr("No !"),  QString(), 1, 1);
    if (status == 0) {
        int rowCount = model->rowCount();
        model->removeRows(0, rowCount);
    }
}
```

As usual, the parent object is pointed to by `this`. The second parameter is the title of the dialog box and the string of the question follows. We shall make the first option verbose by passing **Yes, Delete all records**. The user, upon reading, will know what effect the clicking of the button will have. The **No !** parameter will be displayed on the button that represents the other answer to the question. `QString()` is being passed so that we don't display the third button. When the first button is clicked, 0 will be returned to `status`. When the second button or option is clicked, 1 will be returned. By specifying 1, we make the "`No !`" button the default button of the dialog box. We select 1 again, as the last parameter specifies that "`No !`" should be the button selected when the escape button is pressed.

If the user clicks on the **Yes, Delete all records** button, then status will store 0. In the body of the `if` statement, we obtain the number of rows in our model object. A call to `removeRows` is made and we specify that all the entries from the first, represented by 0, to the `rowCount`, should be removed. However, if the user clicks on the **No !** button, the application will do nothing, as we don't specify that in the `if` statement.

The dialog window should appear as follows when the **Clear All** button is clicked:

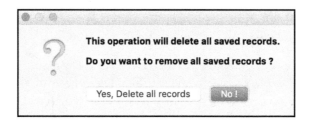

The `saveButtonClicked()` slot has also been modified to show a simple message to the user that the operation has been successful, as demonstrated in the following block of code:

```
void MainWindow::saveButtonClicked()
{
    QStandardItem *name = new QStandardItem(nameLineEdit->text());
    QStandardItem *dob = new
QStandardItem(dateOfBirthEdit->date().toString());
    QStandardItem *phoneNumber = new
QStandardItem(phoneNumberLineEdit->text());
    model->appendRow({ name, dob, phoneNumber});
    clearFields();
    QMessageBox::information(this, tr("RMS System"), tr("Record saved
successfully!"),
                            QMessageBox::Ok|QMessageBox::Default,
                            QMessageBox::NoButton, QMessageBox::NoButton);

}
```

The two last parameters are constants that prevent buttons from showing in the message box.

To allow the application to remove certain rows from the table, the `deleteSaveRecords()` method is used to raise an input-based dialog box that receives the `rowId` of the row we want to remove through the model:

```
void MainWindow::deleteSavedRecord()
{
    bool ok;
    int rowId = QInputDialog::getInt(this, tr("Select Row to delete"),
tr("Please enter Row ID of record (Eg. 1)"),
    1, 1, model->rowCount(), 1, &ok );
    if (ok)
    {
        model->removeRow(rowId-1);
    }
}
```

The `this` keyword refers to the parent object. The second parameter to the call of the static method `QInputDialog::getInt()` is used as the title of the dialog window. The request is captured in the second parameter. The third parameter here is used to specify the default number of the input field. `1`, and `model->rowCount()`, are the minimum and maximum values that should be accepted.

The last but one parameter, `1`, is the incremental step between the minimum and maximum value. `True` or `False` will be stored in `&ok`. When the user clicks **OK**, `True` will be stored in `&ok` and, based on that, the `if` statement will call the `removeRow` on the model object. Whatever value that the user inputs will be passed to `rowId`. We pass `rowId-1` to get the actual index of the row in the model.

The connection to this slot is made by executing the following command:

```
connect(deleteOneEntryToolBarAction, SIGNAL(triggered()), this,
SLOT(deleteSavedRecord()));
```

`deleteOneEntryToolBarAction` is the last but one action on the toolbar.

The following screenshot is what will appear when the user clicks on this action:

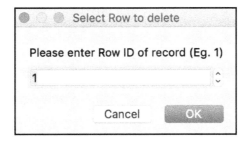

The method that sets up the toolbar is given as follows:

```
void MainWindow::createToolBar() {
    // Setup Tool bar menu
    toolbar = addToolBar("main toolbar");
    // toolbar->setMovable( false );
    newToolBarAction = toolbar->addAction(QIcon(newIcon), "New File");
    openToolBarAction = toolbar->addAction(QIcon(openIcon), "Open File");
    toolbar->addSeparator();
    clearToolBarAction = toolbar->addAction(QIcon(clearIcon), "Clear All");
    deleteOneEntryToolBarAction = toolbar->addAction(QIcon(deleteIcon),
"Delete a record");
    closeToolBarAction = toolbar->addAction(QIcon(closeIcon), "Quit
Application");
}
```

All the other methods are borrowed from the previous section and can be obtained from the source code attached to this book.

To recap, this is what you should see after compiling and running the project:

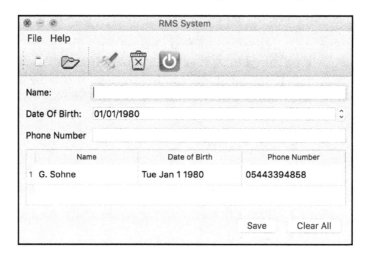

Remember that the reason we already have an entry in the model object is because we created such an entry within the `setupCoreWidgets()` method.

Fill in the name, date of birth, and phone number fields and click on **Save**. This will add an extra line to the table in the window. A dialog message will tell you if the operation was successful.

To delete a row within the table, select the desired row and click on the recycle bin icon, and confirm whether you really want to delete the entry.

Summary

In this chapter, we have seen how to create menus, toolbars, and how to use dialog boxes to receive further input and display information to the user.

In `Chapter 5`, *Managing Events, Custom Signals, and Slots*, we will explore the use of events and more on signals and slots.

5
Managing Events, Custom Signals, and Slots

This chapter introduces the concept of events. To maintain a working state, messages are passed around from the windowing system to the application, and within the application itself. These messages may contain data that could be useful when delivered at some destination. The messages being talked about here are referred to as events in Qt.

In this chapter, we will cover the following topics:

- Events
- Event handlers
- Drag and drop
- Custom signals

Events

In Qt, all events that occur are encapsulated in objects that inherit from the QEvent abstract class. An example of an event that has occurred is when a window has been resized or moved. The change in the state of the application will be noticed, and an appropriate QEvent object will be created to represent it.

The application event loop delivers this object to certain objects that inherit from QObject. This QEvent object is handled by means of a method call that will be invoked.

There are different types of events. When a mouse is clicked, a `QMouseEvent` object is created to represent this. The object will contain additional information, such as the specific mouse button that was clicked, together with the location where that event occurred.

Event handlers

All `QObjects` have an `event()` method that receives events. For `QWidgets`, this method will relay the event object to more specific event handlers. It is possible to redefine what an event handler should do by sub-classing the widget of interest and re-implementing that event handler.

Let's create an application where we shall re-implement an event handler.

Create a folder containing the `main.cpp`, `mainwindow.cpp`, and `mainwindow.h` files. The `mainwindow.h` file should contain the following code:

```
#include <QMainWindow>
#include <QMoveEvent>
#include <QMainWindow>
class MainWindow: public QMainWindow {
    Q_OBJECT
    public:
        MainWindow(QWidget *parent = 0);
    protected:
        void moveEvent(QMoveEvent *event);
};
```

In the preceding code, we have only sub-classed `QMainWindow`. A default constructor is declared and the event handler that we want to override, or re-implement, is the `moveEvent(QMoveEvent *event)` handler.

When a window is moved, the `event()` method of the `QMainWindow` object will be called. The event will be further encapsulated in a `QMoveEvent` object and forwarded to the `moveEvent()` event handler. Since we are interested in changing the behavior of the window when it is moved, we define our own `moveEvent()`.

Add the following lines of code to `mainwindow.cpp`:

```
#include "mainwindow.h"
MainWindow::MainWindow(QWidget *parent) : QMainWindow (parent){
    setWindowTitle("Locate Window with timer");
}
void MainWindow::moveEvent(QMoveEvent *event) {
    int xCord = event->pos().x();
```

```
    int yCord = event->pos().y();
    QString text = QString::number(xCord) + ", " + QString::number(yCord);
    statusBar()->showMessage(text);
}
```

In the default constructor, the title of the window is set. The event object carries the coordinates of where the window currently is. Then `event->pos().x()` is called to obtain the *x* coordinate, likewise the *y* coordinate is obtained by calling `event->pos().y()`.

We convert `yCord` and `xCord` to text and store them in `text`. To access the status bar of the window, `statusBar()` is called and `text` is passed to the `showMessage()` method of the status bar object returned from the call to `statusBar()`.

The `main.cpp` file will contain, as usual, the following code:

```
#include <QApplication>
#include "mainwindow.h"
int main(int argc, char *argv[]){
    QApplication app(argc, argv);
    MainWindow window;
    window.resize(300, 300);
    window.show();
    return app.exec();
}
```

Compile and run the application. Note how the status bar changes when you move the application window.

Here are two screenshots showing how the status bar, located at the bottom of the window, changed when the window was moved.

The first state of the window is shown in the following screenshot:

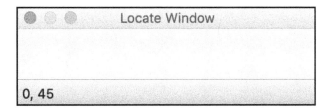

When the window was moved, it later showed the output as shown in the following screenshot:

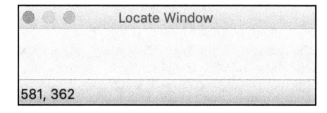

Note the very bottom of the window and how it has changed. Continuously move the window around and observe how the status bar changes.

Let's write another example to improve our understanding of Qt events.

Apart from the events generated by the windowing system, other events are generated by Qt. The example here will illustrate how to tell Qt to send our application timer-based events at certain intervals.

As usual, we shall start with the three main files we usually create, that is, `main.cpp`, `mainwindow.cpp`, and `mainwindow.h`. The project builds upon the previous example.

In the `mainwindow.h` file, insert the following lines of codes:

```
#ifndef MAINWINDOW_H
#define MAINWINDOW_H
#include <QMainWindow>
#include <QMoveEvent>
#include <QMainWindow>
#include <QStatusBar>
#include <QLabel>
class MainWindow: public QMainWindow {
    Q_OBJECT
    public:
        MainWindow(QWidget *parent = 0);
    protected:
        void moveEvent(QMoveEvent *event);
        void timerEvent(QTimerEvent *event);
    private:
        QLabel *currentDateTimeLabel;
};
#endif
```

To receive the timer events, we shall implement our own `timerEvent` method, which will be the destination of the event that is given off when a timer expires. That is the essence of adding the void `timerEvent(QTimerEvent *event)` signature. The `QLabel` `currentDateTimeLabel` instance will be used to display the date and time.

In the `mainwindow.cpp` file, the default constructor is defined by the following code:

```
#include <QDateTime>
#include "mainwindow.h"
MainWindow::MainWindow(QWidget *parent) : QMainWindow (parent){
  setWindowTitle("Locate Window");
  currentDateTimeLabel = new QLabel("Current Date and Time");
  currentDateTimeLabel->setAlignment(Qt::AlignCenter);
  setCentralWidget(currentDateTimeLabel);
  startTimer(1000);
}
```

The title for the window is set. An instance of `QLabel` is created and the call to `setAlignment` ensures that its content says centered. Then `currentDateTimeLabel` is passed to the `setCentralWidget()` method. The `startTimer(1000)` method starts a timer and will trigger a `QTimerEvent` object every second, represented by `1000`.

For each second, we now need to define what should happen by re-implementing the `timerEvent()` method.

Add the following code to `mainwindow.cpp`:

```
void MainWindow::timerEvent(QTimerEvent *event){
    Q_UNUSED(event);
    QString dateTime = QDateTime::currentDateTime().toString();
    currentDateTimeLabel->setText(dateTime);
}
```

Every second, the `timerEvent()` will be called and passed an instance of `QTimerEvent`. The `Q_UNUSED (event)` is used to keep the compiler from complaining that `event()` is not being used in any way. A string representation of the current date and time is passed to `dateTime` and set as the text for the `currentDateTimeLabel` instance variable.

The `main.cpp` file remains the same as before. As a reference it is presented once more, as shown in the following code:

```
#include <QApplication>
#include "mainwindow.h"
int main(int argc, char *argv[]){
    QApplication app(argc, argv);
    MainWindow window;
```

```
    window.resize(300, 300);
    window.show();
    return app.exec();
}
```

Compile and run the application, as shown in the following screenshot:

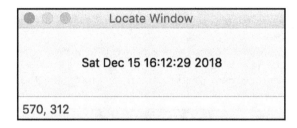

The application will initially show the text, current date, and time, but after a second it should change and display the updated time. Every second that passes will cause text to be updated too.

Drag and drop

In this section, we shall put together a simple application that can handle drag and drop operations from an external source into an application.

The application is a small text editor. When a text file is dropped into the text area, it will open and insert the contents of that text file into the text area. The status of the window will show the number of characters in the text area, which is an instance of a QTextEdit.

This example application also illustrates a very important point about events. To customize a widget, one has to change the existing behavior of that widget by overriding its event handlers. Signals and slots are not considered when trying to customize widgets (except events).

To begin this project, perform the following steps:

1. Create a new folder with a name of your choice
2. Create the main.cpp, mainwindow.cpp, mainwindow.h, dragTextEdit.h, and dragTextEdit.cpp files

The `dragTextEdit.h` and `dragTextEdit.cpp` files will contain the definition of our custom widget. The `mainwindow.cpp` and `mainwindow.h` files will be used to construct the application.

Let's start with the custom `QTextEdit` widget. Insert the following lines of code into `dragTextEdit.h`:

```
#ifndef TEXTEDIT_H
#define TEXTEDIT_H
#include <QMoveEvent>
#include <QMouseEvent>
#include <QDebug>
#include <QDateTime>
#include <QTextEdit>
#include <QMimeData>
#include <QMimeDatabase>
#include <QMimeType>
class DragTextEdit: public QTextEdit
{
    Q_OBJECT
    public:
        explicit DragTextEdit(QWidget *parent = nullptr);
    protected:
        void dragEnterEvent(QDragEnterEvent *event) override;
        void dragMoveEvent(QDragMoveEvent *event) override;
        void dragLeaveEvent(QDragLeaveEvent *event) override;
        void dropEvent(QDropEvent *event) override;
};
#endif
```

The `DragTextEdit` custom widget, inherits from `QTextEdit`. The default constructor is declared. In order to accept a drop event, we need to override the following methods to ensure proper behavior, as shown in the following code:

```
protected:
    void dragEnterEvent(QDragEnterEvent *event) override;
    void dragMoveEvent(QDragMoveEvent *event) override;
    void dragLeaveEvent(QDragLeaveEvent *event) override;
    void dropEvent(QDropEvent *event) override
```

Now that the header file has been created, open the `dragTextEdit.cpp` file and add the definition of the default constructor, as shown in the following code:

```
#include "dragTextEdit.h"
DragTextEdit::DragTextEdit(QWidget *parent) : QTextEdit(parent)
{
    setAcceptDrops(true);
}
```

The `#include` directive imports the header file, after which the default constructor is defined. In order for our widget to accept a drop event, we need to say so by calling the `setAcceptDrops(true)` method.

We now have to add the definition of the methods we want to override. Add the following lines to `dragTextEdit.cpp`:

```
void DragTextEdit::dragMoveEvent(QDragMoveEvent *event)
{
    event->acceptProposedAction();
}
void DragTextEdit::dragLeaveEvent(QDragLeaveEvent *event)
{
    event->accept();
}
void DragTextEdit::dragEnterEvent(QDragEnterEvent *event)
{   event->acceptProposedAction();
}
```

These event handlers deal with the major steps involved when there is going to be a drop action. The `acceptProposedAction()` method is called on the event object in the `dragEnterEvent()` and `dragMoveEvent()` methods. These events are called when the cursor in drag mode is on the boundary of the widget that calls the `setAcceptDrops()` method. If you refuse to call the `acceptProposedAction()` method, the drop behavior may misbehave.

The `dragMoveEvent()` event handler is called when the cursor is within the widget of interest. But to define what happens when the drop event happens we need to define the `dropEvent()` handler.

Add the following code to `dragTextEdit.cpp`:

```cpp
void DragTextEdit::dropEvent(QDropEvent *event)
{
    const QMimeData *mimeData = event->mimeData();
    if (mimeData->hasText()) {
        QTextStream out(stdout);
        QFile file(mimeData->urls().at(0).path());
        file.open(QFile::ReadOnly | QFile::Text);
        QString contents = file.readAll();
        setText(contents);
        event->acceptProposedAction();
    }
    else{
        event->ignore();
    }
}
```

The mime data of the file, encapsulated within the event object, is obtained by calling `event->mimeData()`. If it contains text data, we extract the contents of the file and call the `setText()` method belonging to `QTextEdit`. This will populate the `DragTextEdit` instance with that text. Note the fact that we continue to call `event->acceptProposedAction()` to tell Qt that we have handled this event. If, on the other hand, `event->ignore()` is called, it is taken as an unwanted event or action and is, as such, propagated to a parent widget.

This completes the implementation of custom `QTextEdit`. Now we need to create `mainwindow.h` and `mainwindow.cpp` that will construct the main application window and make use of `DragTextEdit`.

Create the `mainwindow.h` file and insert the following code:

```cpp
#ifndef MAINWINDOW_H
#define MAINWINDOW_H
#include <QMainWindow>
#include <QLabel>
#include <QMoveEvent>
#include <QMouseEvent>
#include <QVBoxLayout>
#include <QDebug>
#include <QDateTime>
#include <QMainWindow>
#include <QStatusBar>
#include "dragTextEdit.h"
class MainWindow: public QMainWindow
{
```

```
    Q_OBJECT
    public:
        MainWindow(QWidget *parent = 0);
    private slots:
        void updateStatusBar();
private:
        DragTextEdit *slateDragTextEdit;
};
#endif
```

The QMainWindow, QLabel class with the other usual classes are imported along with the dragTextEdit.h header file, which allows the inclusion of our custom class. A slot that will be called **anytime text** is added or removed from the DragTextEdit widget and is declared. Lastly, an instance of DragTextEdit is created.

Create and open the mainwindow.cpp file and insert the following code:

```
#include "mainwindow.h"
MainWindow::MainWindow(QWidget *parent) : QMainWindow (parent)
{
    QWidget *mainWidget = new QWidget;
    QVBoxLayout *layout = new QVBoxLayout;
    slateDragTextEdit = new DragTextEdit();
    layout->addWidget(slateDragTextEdit);
    mainWidget->setLayout(layout);
    setCentralWidget(mainWidget);
    statusBar()->showMessage(QString::number(0));
    connect(slateDragTextEdit, SIGNAL(textChanged()), this,
SLOT(updateStatusBar()));
}
void MainWindow::updateStatusBar()
{   int charCount = slateDragTextEdit->toPlainText().count();
    statusBar()->showMessage(QString::number(charCount));
}
```

In the constructor, QWidget and the QVBoxLayout objects are created to hold the main widget and layout. This widget will then be inserted with the call to setCentralWdiget(), as shown in the following code:

```
slateDragTextEdit = new DragTextEdit();
layout->addWidget(slateDragTextEdit);
```

An instance of the `DragTextEdit` custom class is created and passed to `slateDragTextEdit`. This widget is added to our main layout, as shown in the following code:

```
statusBar()->showMessage(QString::number(0));
```

The status bar of the window is set to `0`.

Anytime the `slateDragTextEdit` emits the `textChanged()` signal, a call to the `updateStatusBar()` slot will be called. In this slot, the characters within `slateDragTextEdit` will be extracted and counted. The status bar will thus be updated when a character is added to or removed from `slateDragTextEdit`.

The `main.cpp` file will contain only the following few lines of code to instantiate the window and display it:

```
#include <QApplication>
#include <Qt>
#include "mainwindow.h"
int main(int argc, char *argv[]){
    QApplication app(argc, argv);
    MainWindow window;
    window.setWindowTitle("Drag Text Edit");
    window.show();
    return app.exec();
}
```

At the end of the project, you should have five (5) files in your folder. To compile the project, issue the following commands within the folder on the command line:

```
% qmake -project
```

Don't forget to add `QT += widgets` to the generated `.pro` file. The `.pro` file should contain the header files and program files. It should look like the following code:

```
# Input
HEADERS += dragTextEdit.h mainwindow.h
SOURCES += dragTextEdit.cpp main.cpp mainwindow.cpp
```

Continue to issue the following commands:

```
% qmake
% make
% ./program_executable
```

A running program will look like the following screenshot:

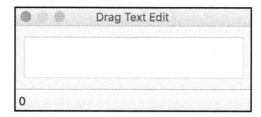

Since there are no characters when the program is executed, the status bar will read **0**, as in the preceding screenshot.

Type some input into the text area and find out how, with every keystroke, the status bar is updated, as we have in the following screenshot:

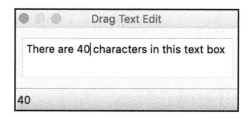

The example in this section illustrates how the text area can accept items external to the application. Drag and drop any text (`.txt`) file, or any file containing text, onto the text area and see how its content is used to populate the textbox, as shown in the following screenshot:

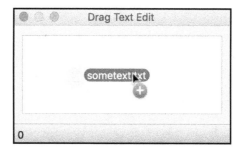

From the preceding screenshot, the content of the `sometext.txt` file, which contains text, will be pasted into the text area as shown in the following screenshot:

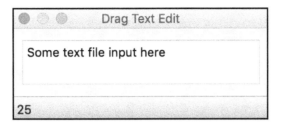

Experiment by removing the call to `acceptProposedAction()` and `accept()` and see how the drag and drop changes.

The last section of this chapter will touch on the creation of a custom signal.

Custom signals

In previous chapters, we saw how to use slots and create custom slots to implement some functionality in response to a signal being emitted. Now, in this section, we will look at how to create custom signals that can be emitted and connected to other slots.

To create a custom signal, one needs to declare a method signature and mark it as a signal with the aid of the `Q_OBJECT` macro. When declared, signals don't have a return type, but they can accept parameters.

Let's get our feet wet with a project. As usual, a new folder should be created with the three (3) files, namely, `main.cpp`, `mainwindow.cpp`, and `mainwindow.h`.

In this example, we shall override `mousePressEvent` and emit a custom signal that will be connected to a slot to perform a number of updates on a window.

In the `mainwindow.h` file, insert the following lines of code:

```
#ifndef MAINWINDOW_H
#define MAINWINDOW_H
#include <QMainWindow>
#include <QMoveEvent>
#include <QMouseEvent>
#include <QVBoxLayout>
#include <QDebug>
#include <QDateTime>
#include <QStatusBar>
```

```
#include <QLabel>
class MainWindow: public QMainWindow
{
    Q_OBJECT
    public slots:
        void updateMousePosition(QPoint pos);
    signals:
        void mouseMoved(QPoint pos);
    public:
        MainWindow(QWidget *parent = 0);
    protected:
        void mousePressEvent(QMouseEvent *event);
    private:
        QLabel *mousePosition;
        QWidget *windowCentralWidget;
};
#endif
```

The custom signal here is declared with the following lines:

```
signals:
    void mouseMoved(QPoint pos);
```

When this signal is emitted, it will pass an instance of QPoint as an argument. If we didn't want our signal to pass any argument, it would have been written with as void mouseMoved().

 Custom signals should return nothing. The signal will be emitted when we re-implement the mousePressEvent() handler.

The void updateMousePosition(QPoint pos), slot will be connected to the custom signal. Its definition is found in mainwindow.cpp.

The member pointer, mousePosition, will display the coordinates of the mouse when it is clicked.

In the mainwindow.cpp file, we shall define three (3) methods. These are the default constructor, the slot updateMousePosition(), and the mousePressEvent() override methods, as shown in the following code:

```
#include "mainwindow.h"
void MainWindow::mousePressEvent(QMouseEvent *event){
    emit mouseMoved(event->pos());
}
```

The `include` statement has to be at the very top of the file. In this `override` method, we obtain the coordinate where the mouse press event was generated by calling `event->pos()`.

The points `x` and `y` coordinates are obtained by calling `x()` and `y()`, respectively.

The `emit mouseMoved(event->pos())` line is used to emit the signal we declared in the header file. Furthermore, `event->pos()` will return a `QPoint` object, which conforms with the signature of the signal.

The following screenshot shows how the slot is defined in the `mainwindow.cpp` file:

```
void MainWindow::updateMousePosition(QPoint point){
    int xCord = point.x();
    int yCord = point.y();
    QString text = QString::number(xCord) + ", " + QString::number(yCord);
    mousePosition->setText(text);
    statusBar()->showMessage(text);
}
```

The `QPoint` instance is received by the slot as a parameter. It's `x` and `y` coordinates are obtained by calling `point.x()` and `point.y()`, respectively. A `QString` instance `text` is used to concatenate the two values, `xCord` and `yCord`, into a longer string.

The `QLabel` instance, `mousePosition`, will be used to display this coordinate by calling its `setText()` method. Similarly, the status bar of the window will be set by calling `statusBar()->showMessage(text)`.

To do the plumbing of connecting the custom signal to our slot, we need to define the default constructor. Add the following lines to `mainwindow.cpp`:

```
MainWindow::MainWindow(QWidget *parent) : QMainWindow (parent){
    windowCentralWidget = new QWidget();
    mousePosition = new QLabel("Mouse Position");
    QVBoxLayout *innerLayout = new QVBoxLayout();
    innerLayout->addWidget(mousePosition);
    windowCentralWidget->setLayout(innerLayout);
    setCentralWidget(windowCentralWidget);
    statusBar()->showMessage("Ready");
    connect(this, SIGNAL(mouseMoved(QPoint)), this,
SLOT(updateMousePosition(QPoint)));
}
```

Like we have been doing, the `windowCentralWidget` is used as the main widget in our application. `QLabel` is added to its layout, `innerLayout`. The status bar is given an initial value of `"Ready"`.

The `mouseMoved(QPoint)` signal is connected to the `updateMousePosition(QPoint)` slot.

In the `main.cpp` file, we shall instantiate our window and start the main event loop, as shown in the following code:

```
#include <QApplication>
#include <Qt>
#include "mainwindow.h"
int main(int argc, char *argv[]){
    QApplication app(argc, argv);
    MainWindow window;
    window.resize(300, 300);
    window.setWindowTitle("Hover Events");
    window.show();
    return app.exec();
}
```

Compile and run the executable, as shown in the following screenshot:

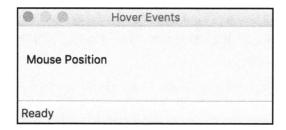

The status bar reads **Ready**, while the `QLabel` making up the main widget in the window reads **Mouse Position**. Now, click on any part within the window, and see the status bar and label change to display the coordinates of the mouse where the click was generated.

See the following screenshot as an example:

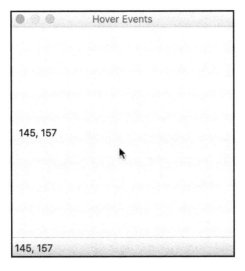

The location of the cursor is **145, 157**, where **145** is on the *x* axis and **157** is on the *y* axis. When the cursor is moved, this value will not change. However, when the mouse is clicked, the `mouseMoved()` signal will be emitted along with the coordinates to update the screen.

Summary

This chapter shed more light on how to use events in Qt. We understood the different situations that call for the use of events instead of the signal-slot mechanism. The first examples touched on how to override and implement custom event handlers. The events we implemented captured the position of a window and also redefined what should happen every second in an example application.

With the aid of events, we also implemented a simple drop event in the drag and drop action, where a simple text editor was created to accept files that are dropped in the text area. Lastly, the chapter illustrated how to create a custom signal that is emitted when an event occurs.

In Chapter 6, *Connecting Qt with Databases*, we will focus on the various ways to store data and retrieve it when building Qt applications.

6
Connecting Qt with Databases

In recent times, most applications integrate with some database for storing information for further processing and future use.

Qt comes with modules and classes that make connecting to databases effortless. The MySql database will be used to illustrate the examples in this chapter, but the same principles will apply to other databases.

By the end of this chapter, you should be able to perform the following:

- Connect and read from a database
- Display and edit database entries via widgets

QtSql

The QtSql module comes equipped with classes and drivers for accessing databases. To proceed beyond this point, you should have made the necessary configuration during the installation of Qt on your system to enable database access.

For those on the macOS using Homebrew, remember to issue the command as previously described in `Chapter 1`, *Introducing Qt 5*.

Linux users have to install the modules and enable the correct flags during compilation to make the QtSql module work, but, for the most part, the instructions in `Chapter 1`, *Introducing Qt 5*, should suffice.

The QtSql module is comprised of the following layers:

- UI layer
- SQL API layer
- Driver layer

User interface level	QSqlQueryModel, QSqlTableModel, QSqlRelationalTableModel
SQL API level	QSqlDatabase, QSqlQuery, QSqlError, QSqlField, QSqlIndex, QSqlRecord
Driver level	QSqlDriver, QSqlDriverCreatorBase, QSqlDriverPlugin, QSqlResult

Each level makes use of classes, as illustrated in the preceding diagram.

Making the connection

We need to set the grounds for writing our applications, and, in this case, we need to have a running instance of MySql. XAMPP is a good candidate to install to have quick access to a working database.

XAMPP is a free and open source, cross-platform web server solution stack package developed by Apache Friends, consisting mainly of the Apache HTTP Server, MariaDB (or MySql) database, and interpreters for scripts written in the PHP and Perl programming languages. Download the latest version from `https://www.apachefriends.org/download.html`.

Let's create a database with the following tables by issuing the following statements:

```
use contact_db;
  CREATE TABLE IF NOT EXISTS contacts (
  id INT AUTO_INCREMENT,
  last_name VARCHAR(255) NOT NULL,
  first_name VARCHAR(255) NOT NULL,
  phone_number VARCHAR(255) NOT NULL,
  PRIMARY KEY (id)
) ENGINE=INNODB;
```

The name of the database is `contact_db`, and it is assumed that you have created it in the MySql instance you installed.

The SQL statements create a table called `contacts` with an auto-increment `id` field along with, `last_name`, `first_name`, and `phone_number` fields that store characters.

Now, create a new folder and add a file called `main.cpp`. Insert the following lines of code:

```
#include <QApplication>
#include <QtSql>
#include <QDebug>
/*
 use contact_db;
   CREATE TABLE IF NOT EXISTS contacts (
   id INT AUTO_INCREMENT,
   last_name VARCHAR(255) NOT NULL,
   first_name VARCHAR(255) NOT NULL,
   phone_number VARCHAR(255) NOT NULL,
   PRIMARY KEY (id)
) ENGINE=INNODB;
*/
int main(int argc, char *argv[]) {
   // Setup db connection
   QSqlDatabase db_conn =
         QSqlDatabase::addDatabase("QMYSQL", "contact_db");
   db_conn.setHostName("127.0.0.1");
   db_conn.setDatabaseName("contact_db");
   db_conn.setUserName("root");
   db_conn.setPassword("");
   db_conn.setPort(3306);
```

```
    // Error checks
    if (!db_conn.open()) {
        qDebug() << db_conn.lastError();
        return 1;
    } else {
        qDebug() << "Database connection established !";
    }
}
```

To make database connections, we need to include QtSql. QDebug provides an output stream where we can write out useful (debugging) information during development to file, device, or standard output.

In the preceding code, the structure of the database table has been commented out, but serves as a reminder in case you have not created it.

To open a connection to a database, a call to QSqlDatabase::addDatabase() is made. The QMYSQL parameter is the driver type, and contact_db is the connection name. A program can have a number of connections to the same database. Furthermore, the addDatabase() call will return an instance of QSqlDatabase, which, in essence, is the connection to the database.

This connection, db_conn, is then initialized with the parameters to make the connection work. The hostname, specific database we want to connect to, username, password, and port number are set on the database connection object, db_conn:

```
db_conn.setHostName("127.0.0.1");
db_conn.setDatabaseName("contact_db");
db_conn.setUserName("root");
db_conn.setPassword("");
db_conn.setPort(3306);
```

Depending on a number of situations, you may need to specify more than these parameters to gain access to a database, but, for the most part, this should work. Also, note that the password is an empty string. It is only for illustration purposes. You have to change the password as pertains to your database.

To make the connection, we need to call open() on the connection object:

```
    // Error checks
    if (!db_conn.open()) {
        qDebug() << db_conn.lastError();
        return 1;
    } else {
        qDebug() << "Database connection established !";
    }
```

A call to `open()` will result in a bool being returned to determine whether the connection to the database was successful. `!db_conn.open()` tests whether the return value is `False`.

Note the way in which we shall compile and run this program.

Issue the following on the command line while you are in the folder where the `main.cpp` file is locate:

```
% qmake -project
```

Open the resulting `.pro` file, and add the following lines:

```
QT += widgets sql
```

We intend to use widgets in the course of this chapter, so it has been listed as the first module to be included. Likewise, we include the SQL module. Proceed with the following commands:

```
% qmake
% make
% ./program_executable
```

If you get the `Database connection established!` response, then it means your program is able to connect to the database smoothly. On the other hand, you may get an error, which will describe the reason why the connection is unable to be established. Go through the following list to ensure you are on the right path when you encounter an error:

- Ensure the database service is running
- Ensure the database you are trying to connect actually exists
- Ensure the table given by the schema exists
- Ensure the username and password for the database exists
- Ensure the Qt was compiled with the MySql module

Now, let's update the program so that we can illustrate how to issue the various SQL statements in Qt.

Listing records

In order to execute query statements against the database, we shall make use of the `QSqlQuery` class. These statements include data-altering statements, such as `INSERT`, `SELECT`, and `UPDATE`. Data definition statements such as `CREATE TABLE` can also be issued.

Consider the following snippet of code to list all entries within the contacts table:

```
QSqlQuery statement("SELECT * FROM contacts", db_conn);
QSqlRecord record = statement.record();
while (statement.next()){
   QString firstName =
statement.value(record.indexOf("first_name")).toString();
   QString lastName =
statement.value(record.indexOf("last_name")).toString();
   QString phoneNumber =
statement.value(record.indexOf("phone_number")).toString();
   qDebug() << firstName << " - " << lastName << " - " << phoneNumber;
}
```

The query statement and the database connection are passed as parameters to an instance of the QSqlQuery statement. QSqlRecord is used to encapsulate a database row or view. We shall use its instance, record, to get the index of a column in a row. statement.record() returns field information for the current query.

If there are any rows that match the query in statement, statement.next() will allow us to cycle through the returned rows. We can call previous(), first(), and last() to enable us to move back and forth with the returned rows or data.

For each row that is returned and accessed by calling statement.next(), the statement object is used to get its corresponding data according to the code, statement.value(0).toString(). This should return the first column in the row converted to string to be stored in firstName. Instead of this approach, we can use record, to obtain the index of the column we are interested in. As such, to extract the first name column, we write statement.value(record.indexOf("first_name")).toString().

The qDebug() call helps to print out the data in firstName, lastName, and phoneNumber, similar to what we would have done using cout.

The INSERT operation

To effect a database operation to store data into the database, there are a number of ways to issue out the INSERT statement.

Consider one form of the INSERT operation in Qt:

```
// Insert new contacts
QSqlQuery insert_statement(db_conn);
insert_statement.prepare("INSERT INTO contacts (last_name, first_name,
```

```
phone_number)"
                              "VALUES (?, ?, ?)");
insert_statement.addBindValue("Sidle");
insert_statement.addBindValue("Sara");
insert_statement.addBindValue("+14495849555");
insert_statement.exec();
```

The QSqlQuery object, insert_statement, is instantiated by passing the database connection. Next, the INSERT statement string is passed to a call to prepare(). Notice how incomplete our statement is with the use of the three (3) ?, ?, ? (question marks). These question marks will be used as placeholders. To fill these placeholders, the addBindValue() method is called. The line, insert_statement.addBindValue("Sidle"), will be used to fill the data in the last_name column of the contacts table. The second call to addBindValue("Sara") will be used to fill the second placeholder.

To execute the statement, the insert_statement.exec() must be called. The overall effect is that a new record will be inserted into the table.

To change the order in which the data is inserted, we can use the insert_statement.bindValue() function instead. The INSERT statement has three (3) positional placeholders, which number from 0 up to 2. We can fill the last placeholder first by specifying it as follows:

```
insert_statement.prepare("INSERT INTO contacts (last_name, first_name,
phone_number)"
                              "VALUES (?, ?, ?)");
insert_statement.bindValue(2, "+144758849555");
insert_statement.bindValue(1, "Brass");
insert_statement.bindValue(0, "Jim");
insert_statement.exec();
```

The placeholder for the phone number column is filled first by specifying bind(2, "+144758849555"), where 2 is the index of the (phone_number) placeholder.

An alternative to using the positions of the placeholders would be to name them. Consider the following INSERT statement:

```
insert_statement.prepare("INSERT INTO contacts (last_name, first_name,
phone_number)"
                              "VALUES (:last_name, :first_name, :phone_number)");
insert_statement.bindValue(":last_name", "Brown");
insert_statement.bindValue(":first_name", "Warrick");
insert_statement.bindValue(":phone_number", "+7494588594");
insert_statement.exec();
```

Instead of using the index of the position when completing the SQL statement, named placeholders are used to reference the data in the VALUES part. That way, the name of the placeholders are passed with a corresponding value to every call to bindValue().

To persist the data, the insert_statement.exec() function must be called.

The DELETE operation

The DELETE operation is another operation that can be performed on a table. To do so, we shall pass a reference to the database connection and pass the DELETE statement to the exec() method of QSqlQuery.

Consider the following snippet:

```
// Delete a record
QSqlQuery delete_statement(db_conn);
delete_statement.exec("DELETE FROM contacts WHERE first_name = 'Warrick'");
qDebug() << "Number of rows affected: " <<
delete_statement.numRowsAffected();
```

numRowsAffected() is a method that is used to figure out how many records were affected. One benefit of this method is that it helps determine whether our query has changed the database. If it returns −1, it means that the query's operation produced indeterminate results.

The UPDATE operation

The UPDATE operation follows the same logic as the DELETE operation. Consider the following lines of code:

```
// Update a record
QSqlQuery update_statement(db_conn);
update_statement.exec("UPDATE contacts SET first_name='Jude' WHERE id=1 ");
qDebug() << "Number of rows affected: " <<
update_statement.numRowsAffected();
```

The statement here sets the first_name of the record with an ID of 1 to 'Jude'. update_statement.numRowsAffected() will return nothing, especially in the case where the first record in the table with id=1 is missing. Do take note of this.

The full program to illustrate the major operations is outlined as follows:

```cpp
#include <QApplication>
#include <QtSql>
#include <QDebug>
int main(int argc, char *argv[]) {
    // Setup db connection
    QSqlDatabase db_conn =
            QSqlDatabase::addDatabase("QMYSQL", "contact_db");
    db_conn.setHostName("127.0.0.1");
    db_conn.setDatabaseName("contact_db");
    db_conn.setUserName("root");
    db_conn.setPassword("");
    db_conn.setPort(3306);
    // Error checks
    if (!db_conn.open()) {
        qDebug() << db_conn.lastError();
        return 1;
    } else {
        qDebug() << "Database connection established !";
    }
    // Create table
    QString table_definition = "use contact_db;\n"
                               "   CREATE TABLE IF NOT EXISTS contacts (\n"
                               "   id INT AUTO_INCREMENT,\n"
                               "   last_name VARCHAR(255) NOT NULL,\n"
                               "   first_name VARCHAR(255) NOT NULL,\n"
                               "   phone_number VARCHAR(255) NOT NULL,\n"
                               "   PRIMARY KEY (id)\n"
                               ")  ENGINE=INNODB;";
    QSqlQuery table_creator(table_definition, db_conn);
    // Issue SELECT statement
    QSqlQuery statement("SELECT * FROM contacts", db_conn);
    QSqlRecord record = statement.record();
    while (statement.next()){
        QString firstName =
        statement.value(record.indexOf("first_name")).toString();
        QString lastName =
        statement.value(record.indexOf("last_name")).toString();
        QString phoneNumber =
        statement.value(record.indexOf("phone_number")).toString();
        qDebug() << firstName << " - " << lastName << " - " <<
        phoneNumber;
    }
    // Insert new contacts
    QSqlQuery insert_statement(db_conn);
    insert_statement.prepare("INSERT INTO contacts (last_name,
    first_name, phone_number)"
```

```
                                    "VALUES (?, ?, ?)");
insert_statement.addBindValue("Sidle");
insert_statement.addBindValue("Sara");
insert_statement.addBindValue("+14495849555");
insert_statement.exec();
//QSqlQuery insert_statement(db_conn);
insert_statement.prepare("INSERT INTO contacts (last_name,
first_name, phone_number)"
                                    "VALUES (?, ?, ?)");
insert_statement.bindValue(2, "+144758849555");
insert_statement.bindValue(1, "Brass");
insert_statement.bindValue(0, "Jim");
insert_statement.exec();
insert_statement.prepare("INSERT INTO contacts (last_name,
first_name, phone_number)"
                                    "VALUES (:last_name, :first_name,
                                    :phone_number)");
insert_statement.bindValue(":last_name", "Brown");
insert_statement.bindValue(":first_name", "Warrick");
insert_statement.bindValue(":phone_number", "+7494588594");
insert_statement.exec();
// Delete a record
QSqlQuery delete_statement(db_conn);
delete_statement.exec("DELETE FROM contacts WHERE first_name =
'Warrick'");
qDebug() << "Number of rows affected: " <<
delete_statement.numRowsAffected();
// Update a record
QSqlQuery update_statement(db_conn);
update_statement.exec("UPDATE contacts SET first_name='Jude' WHERE
id=1 ");
qDebug() << "Number of rows affected: " <<
update_statement.numRowsAffected();
}
```

Of particular importance is how the database table is created. From the preceding code listing, the `QString` instance, `table_definition`, holds the structure of the table we are about to create. The table is created when `table_definition` and the database connection are passed to an instance of `QSqlQuery`. That's all it takes to create a table.

Compile and run the program.

 Remember to edit the `.pro` file to include the `sql` module.

A typical output of the program run from the command is given as follows:

```
./dbBasics.app/Contents/MacOS/dbBasics
Database connection established !
"Jude"  –  "Sidle"  –  "+14495849555"
"Brass"  –  "Jim"  –  "+144758849555"
Number of rows affected:  1
Number of rows affected:  0
```

Using a data model for database access

There are two classes that can be used in accessing the database. These are the QSqlTableModel and QSqlQueryModel classes. The QSqlQueryModel class only provides a read-only model to the database. QSqlTableModel provides both read and write model access to the database.

In application development, you are confronted with the challenge of how to present data and to maintain a relationship between data and presentation (view) such that changes to the data are reflected in the view.

In the early days of the PHP language, data, presentation, and business logic were all jumbled up in one or more scripts. This made debugging and eventual code maintenance a nightmare. This same dilemma does crop up from time to time in language and framework design.

The **Model-View-Controller** (**MVC**) approach is an attempt to solve this problem. It recognizes that one critical piece of software is data. By recognizing this, it abstracts the data into what is called a model. A model is basically a representation of the data in a software. This data can be a list of strings or integers. It can be the folders and files under a parent folder. The data can also be a list of rows that have been returned from a query against a database.

This data that has been obtained needs to displayed or presented to the user. The component(s) through which the data is piped is called the view. For example, an HTML page showing a list of student names can be called a view. In Qt, there are a number of widgets that can be used to display data in a model. Some typical views for data presentation are as follows:

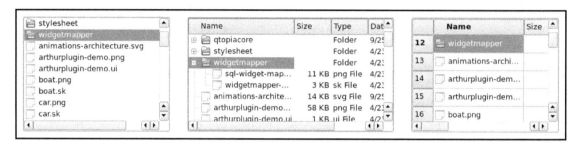

These view classes are optimized for the displaying of information such that, when they are associated with a model, a change in the model will cause the view to be automatically updated. The view maintains its own state and gets informed when there are changes in the model.

For instance, when a list of names is displayed in a `QListView`, a call to `remove()` on the model will both remove the item from the model's list and also update the view by reducing the number of items on display.

Instead of writing code to update the view, the view class does so on our behalf. Let's create a sample project that will make use of a model to access data from a database:

Create a new folder and, within it, create a file named `main.cpp`. Copy over the following lines of code into `main.cpp`:

```cpp
#include <QtSql>
#include <QDebug>
/*
int main(int argc, char *argv[])
{
    // Setup db connection
    QSqlDatabase db_conn =
            QSqlDatabase::addDatabase("QMYSQL", "contact_db");
    db_conn.setHostName("127.0.0.1");
    db_conn.setDatabaseName("contact_db");
    db_conn.setUserName("root");
    db_conn.setPassword("");
    db_conn.setPort(3306);
    // Error checks
```

```cpp
    if (!db_conn.open()) {
        qDebug() << db_conn.lastError(); return 1;
    }
    // Use Database model
    QSqlTableModel *contactsTableModel = new QSqlTableModel(0, db_conn);
    contactsTableModel->setTable("contacts");
    contactsTableModel->select();
    for (int i = 0; i < contactsTableModel->rowCount(); ++i) {
        QSqlRecord record = contactsTableModel->record(i);
        QString id = record.value("id").toString();
        QString last_name = record.value("last_name").toString();
        QString first_name = record.value("first_name").toString();
        QString phone_number = record.value("phone_number").toString();
        qDebug() << id  << " : " << first_name << " : " << last_name << " :
" << phone_number;
    }
    // Insert Row
    int row = contactsTableModel->rowCount();
    contactsTableModel->insertRows(row, 1);
    contactsTableModel->setData(contactsTableModel->index(row, 1),
"Stokes");
    contactsTableModel->setData(contactsTableModel->index(row, 2), "Nick");
    contactsTableModel->setData(contactsTableModel->index(row, 3),
"+443569948");
    contactsTableModel->submitAll();
    // Custom filter
    qDebug() << "\nCustom filter: \n";
    contactsTableModel->setFilter("id=12 AND last_name like'Stokes'");
    contactsTableModel->select();
    for (int i = 0; i < contactsTableModel->rowCount(); ++i) {
        QSqlRecord record = contactsTableModel->record(i);
        QString id = record.value("id").toString();
        QString last_name = record.value("last_name").toString();
        QString first_name = record.value("first_name").toString();
        QString phone_number = record.value("phone_number").toString();
        qDebug() << id  << " : " << first_name << " : " << last_name << " :
" << phone_number;
    }
}
```

The purpose of this program is to connect to a database, list the rows in a particular table, and issue a SELECT statement against it.

After establishing a connection to the database, we create an instance of `QSqlTableModel` with the line, `QSqlTableModel *contactsTableModel = new QSqlTableModel(0, db_conn);`. This instance receives as arguments a pointer to a parent object and a connection to the database connection. This `QSqlTableModel` model allows for editing of the rows in a table too.

To select the table within the database we wish to manipulate, a call to the `setTable()` method is called on `contactsTableModel`. The `contacts` string is passed as the name of the table.

To populate the `contactsTableModel` model with the information in the table, a call to `select()` is issued. A loop is now used to iterate over the data in the model:

```
for (int i = 0; i < contactsTableModel->rowCount(); ++i) {
    QSqlRecord record = contactsTableModel->record(i);
    QString id = record.value("id").toString();
    QString last_name = record.value("last_name").toString();
    QString first_name = record.value("first_name").toString();
    QString phone_number = record.value("phone_number").toString();
    qDebug() << id << " : " << first_name << " : " << last_name << " : " <<
phone_number;
}
```

Each row in the table is obtained by using an index. An index of 0 here refers to the first item in the model. This index is not tied to the **primary key** in the table. It is instead a simple way to reference the rows in the table.

The `rowCount()` method is useful as it helps in knowing the total row count associated with the latest SELECT statement.

To obtain each row in the table, the index in the loop, `i`, is passed to `contactsTableModel->record(i)`. The `QSqlRecord` instance will hold a reference to a row in the table, which was returned by calling `record(i)`.

For each row, the value stored at the intersecting column is obtained by passing the name of the column to `value`. As such, `record.value("id")` will return the value stored in the column `id` of the contact table. `toString()` returns the output as a string. This same call is issued to obtain the values for `last_name`, `first_name`, and `phone_number` for each row (`QSqlRecord` record) in the table.

The `qDebug()` statement is then used to output all the values for each row.

Since `QSqlTableModel` allows for editing of the table, the following statement inserts a new row with data:

```
// Insert Row
int row = contactsTableModel->rowCount();
contactsTableModel->insertRows(row, 1);
contactsTableModel->setData(contactsTableModel->index(row, 1), "Stokes");
contactsTableModel->setData(contactsTableModel->index(row, 2), "Nick");
contactsTableModel->setData(contactsTableModel->index(row, 3),
"+443569948");
contactsTableModel->submitAll();
```

The total items in the table are obtained by calling `rowCount()`. To insert a single row into the table, a call to `insertRows(row, 1)` is made. The single row here is represented by 1 at position `row`.

At column 1, the `last_name` column of the new row gets the value `"Stokes"`, after the call to `setData()`. `contactsTableModel->index(row,1)` represents the index where `"Stokes"` is to be inserted.

To persist the data, a call to `submitAll()` is issued. This will write off any changes that are lingering on in memory to the database.

Note at this point that the model has become the interface for accessing the data in the database. We also do not need to know the specific query that the statements map to for the different kinds of database the application talks to. This is a huge advantage.

If this model were associated with a view, the newly inserted row would be populated onto the screen without any code to perform such an operation.

In order to refine the select statement, the `setFilter()` method is used:

```
// Custom filter
qDebug() << "\nCustom filter: \n";
contactsTableModel->setFilter("id=12 AND last_name like 'Stokes'");
contactsTableModel->select();
```

The `WHERE` clause part of the SQL statement is what is passed to `setFilter()`. The `WHERE` clause, in this case, is selecting rows from the table where the `id` is equal to 12 and the `last_name` field is `'Stokes'`.

To apply the filter, call the `select()` method on `contactsTableModel`. The loop is then used to iterate over the results.

Compile and run the project:

```
% qmake -project
```

Be sure to include the following line in the `.pro` file:

```
QT += sql widgets
```

Compile and run the project:

```
% qmake
% make
% ./executable_file
```

Displaying the model

In the previous section, we saw how to access the database using the model as an abstraction. Now, we shall try to link it with a model for display. Using the code listing from the previous section, modify `main.cpp` to appear as follows:

```cpp
#include <QApplication>
#include <QtSql>
#include <QVBoxLayout>
#include <QPushButton>
#include <QDebug>
#include <Qt>
#include <QTableView>
#include <QHeaderView>
int main(int argc, char *argv[])
{
    QApplication app(argc, argv);
    // Setup db connection
    QSqlDatabase db_conn =
            QSqlDatabase::addDatabase("QMYSQL", "contact_db");
    db_conn.setHostName("127.0.0.1");
    db_conn.setDatabaseName("contact_db");
    db_conn.setUserName("root");
    db_conn.setPassword("");
    db_conn.setPort(3306);
    // Error checks
    if (!db_conn.open()) {
        qDebug() << db_conn.lastError(); return 1;
    }
```

Because we want to display the model, the widgets classes have been included. The database connections remain the same.

Now, add the following lines of code to `main.cpp`:

```
enum {
    ID = 0,
    LastName = 1,
    FirstName = 2,
    PhoneNumber = 3,
};
QSqlTableModel *contactsTableModel = new QSqlTableModel(0, db_conn);
contactsTableModel->setTable("contacts");
contactsTableModel->select();
contactsTableModel->setHeaderData(ID, Qt::Horizontal, QObject::tr("ID"));
contactsTableModel->setHeaderData(LastName, Qt::Horizontal,
QObject::tr("Last Name"));
contactsTableModel->setHeaderData(FirstName, Qt::Horizontal,
QObject::tr("First Name"));
contactsTableModel->setHeaderData(PhoneNumber, Qt::Horizontal,
QObject::tr("Phone Number"));
contactsTableModel->setEditStrategy(
        QSqlTableModel::OnManualSubmit);
```

Instead of using magic numbers such as 0, 1, and so on, enumerators provide some context for the constants 0, 1, and so on.

An instance of `QSqlTableModel` is created using the connection object, `db_conn`. The database table, `contacts`, is selected for operations. When a model is being displayed, headers are used to label the columns. To set this, we pass the enumeration values and the name that the column should bear. For instance, calling `setHeaderData(FirstName, Qt::Horizontal, QObject::tr("First Name"))` will set the first column, `FirstName` (whose real value is 0), to display `"First Name"`, horizontally.

We said that the `Model-View` concept has an added benefit in that changes made to the view can be made to reflect in the database without writing extra code:

```
contactsTableModel->setEditStrategy(
        QSqlTableModel::OnManualSubmit);
```

The preceding lines stipulate that changes to the data displayed in the view should not be propagated to the database. Instead, an independent process should trigger the syncing of the view with the data in the database. In contrast to making the syncing process a manual one, replace the code that has been commented out:

```
//contactsTableModel->setEditStrategy(
//        QSqlTableModel::OnRowChange);
```

`setEditStrategy(QSqlTableModel::OnRowChange)` means that changes made to the data via the view will reflect in the database when the data in the row has changed. We will see more of this when we run the completed program.

Since we have created the model, it is time to add the view. Add the following lines of code to `main.cpp`:

```
//contactsTableModel->setEditStrategy(
//       QSqlTableModel::OnRowChange);
// continue from here ...
QTableView *contactsTableView = new QTableView();
contactsTableView->setModel(contactsTableModel);
contactsTableView->setSelectionMode(QAbstractItemView::SingleSelection);
contactsTableView->setSelectionBehavior(QAbstractItemView::SelectRows);
QHeaderView *header = contactsTableView->horizontalHeader();
header->setStretchLastSection(true);
```

To show the entries in the database table, the view class, `QTableView`, is used here. The `QTableView` class is special in that it is a class with an implementation of a model and view all-in-one. That means that internally, this class has an internal model where data can be inserted for display. For our purposes, we shall replace this model.

`QTableView` presents data in a tabular form with rows and columns. We are choosing to use this view since it resembles how data is organized in a relational database.

After an instance of `QTableView` has been instantiated, we set the model to `contactsTableModel`, which is the model we created by ourselves by calling the `setModel()` method.

The selection of items in the table is restricted to a single item when the `setSelectionMode()` method is called. If we want to allow multiple selections in the table, then the `QAbstractItemView::MultiSelection` constant should be passed to `setSelectionMode()`. The selection, in this case, is made by clicking and dragging the mouse over the items in the table in which you have an interest.

In order to specify what can be selected, the `QAbstractItemView::SelectRows` constant is passed to `setSelectionBehavior()`. This constant allows for only entire rows to be selected.

When `QTableView` is rendered, there is unused space to the right of the widget.

This problem is illustrated in the following screenshot:

Consider how the space marked **Empty space** presents a gaping hole in the interface.

In order to make the last column stretch to fill the containing widget, we need to obtain an instance of the header object of QTableView and set the desired property, setStretchLastSection(), to true, as in the following code:

```
QHeaderView *header = contactsTableView->horizontalHeader();
header->setStretchLastSection(true);
```

At this point, we need to construct a simple window and layout for the application. Add the following lines to main.cpp:

```
QWidget window;
QVBoxLayout *layout = new QVBoxLayout();
QPushButton *saveToDbPushButton = new QPushButton("Save Changes");
layout->addWidget(contactsTableView);
layout->addWidget(saveToDbPushButton);
```

A QVBoxLayout instance will serve as the main layout for the application window. Changes made to the entries in the table will not be persisted to the database. We have intentionally made it thus, in order to use a button to manually write changes to the database. As such, a QPushButton instance is created. The table and button are added to the layout object.

The last lines of code for `main.cpp` are as follows:

```
    QObject::connect(saveToDbPushButton, SIGNAL(clicked()),
contactsTableModel, SLOT(submitAll()));
  window.setLayout(layout);
  window.show();
  return app.exec();
}
```

The `clicked()` signal of the `saveToDbPushButton` object is connected to the `submitAll()` slot of the model, `contactsTableModel`. After making changes to the entries on the table in the application, clicking the **Push** button will write the changes to the database.

The rest of the code reads the same as always.

To compile the application, perform the following commands:

```
% qmake -project
```

Make sure the `QT` variable in the `.pro` file has the following line:

```
QT += widgets sql
```

Continue with the following commands:

```
% qmake
% make
% ./name_of_executable
```

The output of the application will populate a list in the table, assuming the contacts table is not empty:

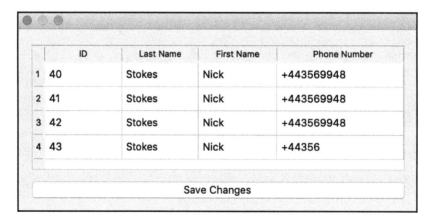

Note how the last column has extended all the way to the edge of the window. From the preceding screenshot, you can see data that has already been persisted in the database. Double-click on any of the cells and edit its content. Click on the **Save Changes** button. When you visit the database, you will see that the changes in the application have been reflected in the app.

Summary

This chapter illustrated how to connect to databases when developing Qt applications. We learned how to use models to serve as an abstraction for manipulating data in a database. Finally, the information in the database table was displayed with the aid of Model-View classes. These classes make it easy to extract data for display, while allowing changes made in the view to be propagated to the database.

Other Books You May Enjoy

If you enjoyed this book, you may be interested in these other books by Packt:

Qt 5 Projects
Marco Piccolino

ISBN: 9781788293884

- Learn the basics of modern Qt application development
- Develop solid and maintainable applications with BDD, TDD, and Qt Test
- Master the latest UI technologies and know when to use them: Qt Quick, Controls 2, Qt 3D and Charts
- Build a desktop UI with Widgets and the Designer
- Translate your user interfaces with QTranslator and Linguist
- Get familiar with multimedia components to handle visual input and output
- Explore data manipulation and transfer: the model/view framework, JSON, Bluetooth, and network I/O
- Take advantage of existing web technologies and UI components with WebEngine

Mastering Qt 5
Guillaume Lazar

ISBN: 9781786467126

- Create stunning UIs with Qt Widget and Qt Quick
- Develop powerful, cross-platform applications with the Qt framework
- Design GUIs with the Qt Designer and build a library in it for UI preview
- Handle user interaction with the Qt signal/slot mechanism in C++
- Prepare a cross-platform project to host a third-party library
- Build a Qt application using the OpenCV API
- Use the Qt Animation framework to display stunning effects
- Deploy mobile apps with Qt and embedded platforms

Leave a review - let other readers know what you think

Please share your thoughts on this book with others by leaving a review on the site that you bought it from. If you purchased the book from Amazon, please leave us an honest review on this book's Amazon page. This is vital so that other potential readers can see and use your unbiased opinion to make purchasing decisions, we can understand what our customers think about our products, and our authors can see your feedback on the title that they have worked with Packt to create. It will only take a few minutes of your time, but is valuable to other potential customers, our authors, and Packt. Thank you!

Index

QtSql module
  about 99
  layers 100
QtSql
  connection, making 100, 101, 102, 103
  DELETE operation 106
  INSERT operation 104, 105
  records, listing 103, 104
  UPDATE operation 106, 108
QVBoxLayout class
  about 27, 28
  reference 21

S

signals
  about 33, 34
  connecting, with slots 35

multiple signals, connecting to single slot 39, 40, 42
single signal, connecting to multiple slots 37, 38, 39
slots 33, 34

W

widgets
  about 15, 17, 19
  key points 15
  laying out 21
Windows
  Qt, installing on 9

X

XAMPP
  download link 100

www.ingramcontent.com/pod-product-compliance
Lightning Source LLC
LaVergne TN
LVHW081529050326
832903LV00025B/1701